I0503981

Table of Contents

Foreword

Acknowledgements

Part I – Introduction

Part II – Trust is Not Your Friend

Part III – Advisors

Part IV – Investing

Part V – High Risk and Fraudulent Investments

Part VI – Planning and Implementation

Part VII – Other Issues and Risks

Part VIII – Monitoring – Watching Out For Avoidable Losses

Part IX – Frequent Elements of Fraud Against Athletes and Celebrities

Conclusion

References

About the Author

Appendix 1 – Basic Concepts

Appendix 2 – Who Does What: the Players

Appendix 3 – Information to Request from Potential Financial Advisors or Managers

Appendix 4 – Researching a Financial Advisor

Appendix 5 – Asset Classes

Appendix 6 – Common Schemes

Appendix 7 – Questionnaire for Investments Being Considered

Appendix 8 – List of Financial Documents to Retain

Foreword

The 2nd edition of *Avoidable Losses: A Guide to Keeping What You've Earned* has been updated to include new material and reorganized to streamline the content.

The book is called *Avoidable Losses* because most significant financial losses suffered by individuals could be avoided. It is intended for professional athletes, entertainers and others **who rely on other people for financial advice and/or financial or business management**. It is not intended as investment advice or legal advice but as education that can help you keep what you've earned.

Most people will do better financially in the long term if they have a good financial adviser. However, if you have bad financial advice or management you need to know now because it can expose you to total financial loss. Helping you to understand the difference between good and bad financial advisors, advice and management is what this book is about.

The book will help you to

- Know what to look for and what steps to take when selecting your advisers and making investments;

- Understand what's important to watch for when others are managing your money and investments;

- Recognize the major risks to your financial security; and

- Know what you can do to reduce your risk of becoming the victim of a major loss.

Being aware of and taking into account the risks discussed in the coming chapters can greatly reduce the risk of losing your money, investments and financial security.

In addition, the Appendices provide reference materials and practical checklists you can use.

- Appendix 1 discusses basic investing concepts.

- Appendix 2 includes explanations of the players in the investing world; good information to know and a good place to turn to with questions.
- Appendix 3 is a checklist illustrating information you should request, and evaluate, from any advisor you are considering.
- Appendix 4 is an approach to researching potential advisors.
- Appendix 5 provides information on various Asset Classes.
- Appendix 6 is description of common schemes.
- Appendix 7 is a questionnaire you should request your advisor to complete for investments recommended to you or under consideration.
- Appendix 8 is an example list of documents you should maintain.

This book provides **practical independent** guidance. Unfortunately, there are so many people in the financial services industry with conflicts of interest who will put their interests ahead of yours, it is hard to know who you should believe. The information in this book is free from those financial industry conflicts and knowing this information will help you protect your wealth and financial security.

Finally I would like to note that throughout the book I have used "he" and "him" rather than "she" and "her". A choice was necessary for ease of writing and the male form was chosen simply because most of the cases of financial losses suffered by athletes and entertainers involve male advisors.

Acknowledgements

Several people were kind enough to give their time either educating me about the realities of life as a professional athlete or reading the manuscript and providing feedback. I would like to thank the following people:

Colin Bagnell, entrepreneur

Jon Earl, Bluedoor Publishing

Jo-Anne Findley, CPA (Canada)

Stanley Jackson, Minnesota Timberwolves Client Development

Len Ritchot, entrepreneur, hockey player and coach

Neil Sheehy, ICE Hockey Agency

John Thomas, National Manager - Ultimate Hoops Training

Your input was truly appreciated.

This is for my wife Ria, daughter Tara and son Ian.

Thanks to Ian for your assistance researching and finding interesting cases and acting as a sounding board.

Special thanks to Tara for all your input and for being my editor.

Part I – Introduction

> **"There's no handbook on how to handle yourself, so you learn some things along the way, and hopefully you don't lose too big." Matt Birk, former Minnesota Viking** [1]

It's one thing to make money, another to keep it. There is no shortage of ways to spend it or lose it and no shortage of people from every walk of life willing to take it off your hands. Like it or not, having money makes you a target of those people.

The main contributing factors to people permanently losing large amounts of their money can be boiled down to three:

1. Fraud and scams;
2. Mismanagement by the advisors, players or both; and
3. Incompetence.

Of course there are many variations of each of these main contributing factors. And many times when there is a significant loss, there are multiple factors. But even though the material in the book focusses mostly on fraud and scams, the approach to reducing the risks from each of these is the same.

There is a fourth contributing factor to losses: a lack of care about what happens to your own money and unwillingness to take steps to prevent losses. I don't think you'd be reading this if you fall into the fourth category.

When an athlete or other celebrity retires and has no money left, too many people immediately point to out-of-control spending as the reason. In some cases this may be the cause, and in many cases it's a factor, but most times no one digs into the records to find out what really happened to the money. Out-of-control spending is just too convenient an explanation that many people are willing to accept; even the victims in many cases.

My belief is this: **if your spending is out-of-control you also aren't paying attention to what is happening with the rest of your money. Others, including agents, advisors and** managers see this and know it makes you an easy target for investment scams, embezzlement, extra fees, and more. When you're an easy target, you'd be surprised how many people who you think you can trust will take advantage of that to part you from your money.

Imagine this scenario after your career: you and your family living comfortably in a beautiful home, no worries about money to pay your bills, able to travel and spend your time doing things you want. If you have kids, you are able to help them attend the best universities. Perhaps you have a charity or other cause you want to support and you can afford to do it.

By following the guidance in this book you can reduce the risks of being one of those people who had it all but lost it. Instead, you can make your money last, you and your family can live the good life, and you can do it without having to constantly worry about your finances.

The First Rule: Don't Lose

Warren Buffett is acknowledged as one of the most successful investors today. His advice for investing and preserving your financial security is:

- **Rule #1 – Don't lose what you have.**

- **Rule #2 – If in doubt, refer to rule #1.**

If you suffer a significant loss, say a million dollars, you lose what you already worked for. This is bad enough by itself, but you also lose the interest or earnings that you should be making on that lost million dollars in the coming years. **Depending on how many years that money could have been earning a return, your loss may well include the original million dollars plus a couple of million more that you would have earned on it if it hadn't been lost.** This is why protecting what you have is so important and why it's worth spending time, energy and money to protect it.

Many people don't understand the risks to their wealth. For instance, people are aware that investing in the stock market can be risky, but generally don't know what "risk" refers to or that they can reduce their risks. As a result many people stay out of the stock market but end up investing in things that are far riskier.

In sports, the best defense is often said to be a good offense. When it comes to protecting your money a good defense starts with understanding enough so that **when you say you want your money invested conservatively, you'll know if it is**.

Permanent vs Temporary Losses

Buffett's First Rule of "don't lose what you have" is the essence of what this book is about, but it is important to understand that when we talk about not losing your wealth we are talking about not suffering large *permanent* losses.

Permanent losses are those related to something you owned but no longer have. For example, let's say that you purchased the home of your dreams. And say it's located in a flood zone and a major hurricane comes and destroys the home, but you find you didn't have insurance coverage because of where it was located. At this point, you your house is gone and you have suffered a permanent loss.

On the other hand, not everything people refer to as a loss is a permanent loss. The best example is the total of all the stocks in the stock market. Many days the combined prices of the shares traded on the stock market will drop. You will hear people say something like, "it was a bad day, the market lost 10% of its value". First, this reference means that the overall market has declined 10%; it doesn't mean the shares of every publicly traded company have gone down 10%; some will have declined more, some less, and possibly some have increased. In this situation, although the stock market has gone down history has shown that with enough time it will recover. If you invested in the entire market, you can be comfortable you only have a temporary loss because the market overall will increase in value again.

Stocks and the stock market will go up and down every day. This is called volatility. In the above scenario, when the markets go down many people give in to fear and sell their investments. This results in a permanent loss.

In contrast to decreases in the entire stock market in the U.S. which will rebound at some time, shares of <u>individual</u> companies can, and do, lose all of their value permanently. For instance, if you had bought shares in a company that went bankrupt (like Enron), the shares become worthless and you would have a permanent loss.

The lesson here is that permanent losses are what really hurt you and that you really need to avoid.

....

Antoine Walker – Avoidable Losses Case #1

Antoine Walker's story is probably somewhat familiar to many people reading this. Walker was a star in the NBA with the Boston Celtics and Miami Heat. He made more than $110 million in salary and endorsements during his NBA career from 1996 through 2008. In 1999 Boston signed him to a six-year, $77 million deal. No-one thought he would be able to go through all that money in his lifetime, but they were wrong. When he finished playing in the NBA he was effectively broke and in May 2010 he filed for bankruptcy.

Walker's first agent was David Falk who sold his agency, FAME, to SFX Entertainment in 1999. It appears that at some point Walker hired SFX Financial Management to provide financial services to him and continued to work with a SFX Financial advisor, Brian Ourand, throughout his NBA career.

Walker lived big. He bought big houses, drove big cars, had a big social circle and a big family, spent big on clothes, and gambled big. Many articles were written blaming Walker's financial troubles on his gambling, out of control spending, and the cost of supporting his friends and extended family. Walker himself has given plenty of examples showing these were factors but, according to Walker, the investments he made were the main reason for his financial downfall.

According to an article, *Antoine Walker educates Alabama football team on financial pitfalls* in the Tuscaloosa News,

> "Walker said if he had it to do over again, he wouldn't personally invest while he was playing.
>
> "I really have no recollection of the things I was investing in, especially in the real estate market". [2]

Walker has said he owned over a hundred properties during his career. Especially in the early 2000's, when housing prices were increasing and apartments were easily rented, purchasing apartment buildings seemed like a smart thing to do. With so much going on, Walker didn't have the time to make all the purchases himself. To make the process easier, Walker and his mother Diane apparently gave Ourand a partial Power of Attorney and then at another time gave him an unlimited Power of Attorney. With the Powers of Attorney Ourand was able to buy properties and take out mortgages on their behalf, leaving them free to do other things.

Initially properties were purchased in Walker's own name. Later companies were set up to purchase and own the properties but he also gave his personal guarantee for the mortgage loans on the properties. It appears that most of the properties he purchased were lower rent apartments in or around Chicago, many of which were in need of repair. Because of his high salary he had no problem borrowing money for these purchases.

In 2004, the housing market peaked and prices that had been propped up by cheap credit began to decline. Eventually this led to the financial crisis of 2007/2008 and banks tightened lending policies to the point where it was almost impossible to get loans. When Walker's NBA career ended in 2008, his income and the apartment rents dropped below what was needed to cover the monthly mortgage payments. He attempted to keep making payments on the mortgages but eventually he was unable to keep up. When he filed for personal bankruptcy the only investments he listed were a few apartment buildings in the Chicago area.

Avoidable Losses?

Were Walker's losses avoidable? As we discuss later, if you don't invest at all, the money you have will lose its value over time because of inflation. The key is to invest without losing your wealth. Unfortunately, Walker's comment that "you should go through a financial advisor, somebody who tells you about a couple of things you should be invested in, and let them lead the way" over-simplifies the task and understates the risk in simply finding an advisor and following his advice.

If you get the right advisory team in place with the right controls and oversight, following their advice makes sense. In reality, there have been far too many cases where the advisor and advisory firm have put their interests ahead of the client or has even been part of a fraudulent scheme to gain control of their client's money. Even an honest advisor can suggest bad investments or a bad strategy leading to significant losses.

It's important that you understand the basics of investing, ask questions, and understand what is happening with your money. If you don't have the time or interest to do that, you need a representative who is totally independent of your financial advisors/ managers/ agent to closely monitor your investments and your other financial assets.

It's interesting that Walker said,

> "I really have no recollection of the things I was investing in, especially in the real estate market." [3]

So how involved was Walker and who was advising him? As noted above, one person who appears to have been quite involved in Walker's affairs was Brian Ourand of SFX Financial. He had Walker's Power of Attorney and was able to sign documents for Walker (and Walker's mother).

The concentration of Walker's investments in real estate was a major mistake that an advisor would be expected to prevent. Why? One key to investing is that **to reduce your risk, you diversify your investments**. Diversification means having many different investments. Through diversification of your investments, you ensure that you aren't exposing all of your investments to the same risks.

Here is a lesson from Walker's story. Diversification is not achieved by buying several less expensive apartment properties rather than one really expensive one. Either way, you are still invested in apartments and they are all subject to the same risks; if something happens in the economy that affects the value of one apartment building, it will affect them all.

Diversification is achieved by dividing your investment dollars between several types, or classes, of investments. This might be dividing your investments between, say, large company stock, small company stock, international stock, company and government bonds, real estate, and possibly other options.

Walker's investments were in the same type of apartment buildings, in the same area, resulting in concentration and very high risk, something that any financial advisor should know to avoid.

I think most people would agree that any undiversified investment strategy would be clearly unsuitable for Walker or any other athlete. Further, the concentration of investments in apartment buildings seems to have been the opposite of what the firm says in a recent brochure which reads,

---

SFX Financial Advisory Management Enterprises, LLC Part 2A of Form ADV

Investment Advisory Services

"Investment advisory services provided by Applicant include preparation of an asset allocation strategy; implementation of a selected investment program utilizing third party managers and open-end mutual funds to meet client's specific investment objectives and risk tolerance; monitoring, reporting and performance review of recommended investments; and periodic rebalancing of investment portfolio in conjunction with client's financial goals."

Whether in their brochure at the time or not, these are basic principles that a client would expect from most firms. However, it doesn't appear the above described actions were implemented in Walker's case. Take this as a lesson: if your investments or investment strategy differs from what your advisory firm says in its printed materials, this should be a cause for concern. It would also suggest a possible lack of supervision by the firm over its advisors, which increases the risk to you.

Walker's initial real estate investments were purchased in his name. If someone got hurt on the property, he would have been open to be sued personally. One of Walker's apartment buildings was said to have bricks falling from it. It's not hard to see the potential for one of these hitting someone and causing permanent injury. If that had happened, it could have resulted in an award in the multi-millions of dollars, which Walker likely would have been on the hook for, because the building was in his name.

The apartment buildings were eventually transferred to or purchased by companies that Walker owned which significantly reduced the risk to Walker's personal wealth, however, to purchase the properties Walker obtained mortgage loans which he personally guaranteed. That meant that if the company he set up to hold the building could not make the mortgage payments from the rents it received, Walker would have to use his personal money to make the mortgage payments (as actually happened). He wouldn't be able to just walk away, keep his money, and let the mortgage company take over the building.

Borrowing money to invest, whether for real estate or other investments, is referred to as leverage. Leverage provides additional funds allowing you to invest more, but it is also a very risky strategy. **It puts you in a position of being exposed to losing more than you invested**. For example, if the value of the real estate goes down, the amount owed on the loans doesn't also go down. In real terms, if you borrowed $500,000 in 2005 and added it to $100,000 you had already saved, you could buy a house for $600,000. When housing values began to decrease in 2007, let's say you could only sell the house for $400,000. Even though you would only receive $400,000 for selling the house, you would still owe the bank the $500,000 you borrowed (leverage) plus interest. As you see, the loan is more than the value of the house, requiring you to use your money or other assets to pay off the remaining $100,000. You have lost your original own cash of $100,000 and also the $100,000 you have to repay the bank. This can, and apparently did for Walker, result in bankruptcy. Utilizing leverage for investing is a very risky strategy and one that is suited to speculation but not to investing for financial security in retirement.

The risk to Walker's wealth was further increased when he gave his advisor an unlimited Power of Attorney ("POA"). On January 1, 2006 it appears that Walker and his mother both gave an unlimited POA to Brian Ourand. An unlimited POA allows the named person to do anything with your money and your credit that you could do. The person could sell your assets, spend or transfer your money, borrow money in your name, buy and sell properties or other investments, and sign documents you would normally sign. In other words, the person you give an unlimited POA to can use your money or properties or cars or good credit to do anything you could do. And you may never find out if they don't want you to.

The risk to Walker's financial security was increased dramatically by not knowing what was happening in his own affairs. In his words, "If you're not there to watch it bad things are going to happen." [4] He didn't watch over what was going on with his finances and was relying far too heavily on his financial advisors who apparently managed his finances.

As happens in many cases of fraud against athletes and entertainers, it appears that his advisors were a one-stop shop managing all or most of his financial affairs. Apparently SFX Financial did Walker's banking, paid his bills, made investments, borrowed money and, presumably, did his accounting and looked after his taxes. **When you allow one person or firm to manage all or most of your financial affairs, without you or someone independent watching what they are doing, it is perhaps the riskiest situation you could create**.

As a side note, Brian Ourand, the financial advisor who worked with Walker, was later named in a lawsuit filed by Mike Tyson alleging that the advisor had embezzled money from Tyson while advising him. Subsequently the U.S. Securities and Exchange Commission ("SEC") instituted cease and desist proceedings against Ourand alleging he stole funds from three clients' accounts at SFX Financial. The other two clients were not identified. The SEC Order stated that,

"From 2006 to 2011, Ourand misappropriated at least $670,000 from clients. During this time, Ourand wrote unauthorized checks from client bank accounts payable to cash or to himself and wired unauthorized amounts to himself for his own personal use. He also wired money using client credit cards for unauthorized amounts to others for their personal use. In addition, Ourand forged a client's name and engaged in other deceptive conduct."

The SEC also instituted cease and desist proceedings against SFX Financial and its Chief Compliance Officer. This was in part because of their failure to follow their own procedures and controls.

Besides Walker's admitted out of control spending, the other factors identified above as creating risks which led to losses could have also been avoided.

Having an understanding of the risks you face and implementing appropriate strategies will significantly reduce your chance of suffering a major loss. The following chapters will cover both risks and strategies.

....

Summary

Warren Buffet is acknowledged as one of the most successful investors today. He has said that the first rule for investing and preserving your financial security is "Don't lose what you have".

Antoine Walker obviously wasted a lot of money but it also appears that he didn't receive good financial management or advice. If he understood the risks and either he or his representative had monitored his finances, he should never have needed to declare bankruptcy. Walker learned that if you hand over your money to someone else to manage and don't monitor what is done with it, bad things happen.

Part II – Trust is Not Your Friend

> *"Lesson number one: Don't underestimate the other guy's greed."*
>
> – Tony Montana (Al Pacino) – "*Scarface*" 1983

Investment Fraud

Investment fraud in the U.S. has been estimated by the FBI at up to $50 billion annually. That's an average of over:

- $136.8 million per day
- $5.7 million per hour
- $95 thousand per minute.

The above figure doesn't take into account many other activities that have been exposed that may well be investment frauds. For example, recently there have been numerous cryptocurrency firms springing up and selling Initial Coin Offerings otherwise known as ICOs. And investment banks, insurance companies and private funds have sold billions of dollars of mortgage backed securities knowing that they were far riskier than they were telling customers.

This much fraud isn't the result of a few people losing money or of only a few fraudsters. It is common.

The point is that fraud is a very real threat to your money and your financial security; a threat that can victimize anyone and relies on gaining your trust.

Advisors They Trusted

> "On a street level, you can see the [hustlers] coming." But "this is white collar--this is something you can't see. It is like a cancer; you don't know until it's there." NFL player Simeon Rice [6]

Financial crimes such as investment fraud and embezzlement are different from street crime or theft. The biggest reason you can't see it, as Simeon Rice says, is because of trust. The most common thing people say when they learn they have been defrauded is, I trusted him! I can't believe it was him!

A lot of well-intentioned articles, blogs and videos advise new professional athletes to find an advisor they trust. Unfortunately that's like advising a beginning golfer to hit the ball down the middle of the fairway. Good advice but without understanding how to do it, it's unlikely to happen.

Telling someone to "Find someone you trust" really is a disservice to them. It suggests that it is easy to do and in some cases that it's all you need to do.

The article excerpts below show how some of the most trusted friends have turned out to be fraudsters, totally without concern for their victims. Unfortunately too many people have to learn this the hard way.

Robert Anglen, The Republic | azcentral.com July 25, 2014

Ricky Johnson said he wanted to attend Brown's sentencing, but he only has about $8,000 left in his savings account.

The 56-year-old Minnesota man said Brown preyed on his emotional weaknesses and used the 2010 suicide of his son to befriend him and lure him into investing.

Johnson said Brown's scheme cost him most of his savings and caused both his daughter and his brother to lose their homes. Johnson said he will carry the shame of investing his family's money with Brown until he dies.

"Ray told me he loved me," he said. "He really is the greatest, greatest, nicest con man in the world." [7]

Howard Ain Updated: Wednesday, July 2 2014

The man behind the scam stole from hundreds of victims. He lured people to an investment with the promise of making millions of dollars. But, instead, they lost everything.

Misty Helms, a fraud victim, said, "I was very angry, very disheartened 'cause I really trusted him."

Misty Helms was crushed to find out she and her husband had lost all of their savings in a bogus investment, "I owned a restaurant and he ate in my restaurant every day. For approximately 30 years I've known this man." [8]

Dan Browning, Star Tribune, May 9, 2012

Jason "Bo" Beckman's mother testified Wednesday in Minneapolis that long before he was accused of defrauding investors in Trevor Cook's $194 million Ponzi scheme, her son had bilked her and her sisters out of much of their inheritance. [9]

Experience has shown many times over that fraudsters will go to great lengths to gain your trust because trust leads to access to your money. There's very little chance that you will see their true character just from talking or spending time with them. **Unless you take steps to independently verify their honesty and integrity, they'll fool you every time.** Blind trust will likely lead you to join the ranks of those who had money and financial security but lost it.

Don't misunderstand; you need a high level of trust in your advisors because you certainly don't want to give any access to your money to someone you don't trust!

The point is that trust isn't just a feeling and isn't to be given easily. Trust should start with understanding the honesty and integrity of the advisor by conducting a thorough background investigation; and then is (hopefully) proved through experience working together. **But even then trust shouldn't be thought of as all you need to protect your financial security.**

Remember the saying, "Trust but verify"? I believe it has to be **"verify before you trust"** when it involves anyone with access to your wealth. Then, trust them to do what you hire them to do, but continue to monitor that they are actually doing what they should. We will discuss ongoing monitoring later.

Whenever you hear someone say they don't need to worry about their money, that they have complete trust in their advisors, take note. The odds are pretty good that person will be a victim sooner or later.

Athletes, Entertainers and Celebrities Are Especially Vulnerable

The player clients of Joseph Vaccaro of New York City's Dynasty Management and Vincent "Vinnie" Porter of Chicago's PTA Sports Management didn't suspect this.

New York Financial Adviser Pleads Guilty to Conspiring to Defraud Professional Athlete Clients

U.S. Attorney's Office, Southern District of California

February 02, 2015

"As part of his plea agreement, Vaccaro admits that over the next few months, he and Porter devised a plot to hoodwink investors by telling them that the Burger King franchises would be purchased for $37 million, when in fact their true value was less than half that amount. The conspirators also concealed the fact that they intended to take millions of dollars "off the top" of the deal, and fraudulently take a 50% ownership interest in the franchises themselves."

"As the conspirators had discussed earlier, however, they actually planned to purchase the franchises for approximately $16 million, and would simply pocket the difference between investors' payments and the actual purchase price."

If this scam hadn't been identified by law enforcement during a separate investigation, it's doubtful those invested in the deal would have seen through the fraud anytime soon; maybe never. Like many others, no doubt.

No one knows the extent of financial crime against the general population or against athletes or entertainers or other celebrities. A big reason is that only some victims will report being defrauded. Many victims are too embarrassed to admit it. Another group of victims, likely a larger group, don't know that they have been victims. People in this second group either (1) don't know what fraud really is; (2) simply accept whatever lies they are told about their losses; (3) don't have the facts of what really happened; or (4) think their money is still safely invested.

We don't even need to know the full extent to know that fraud against individuals and families is a major problem.

Many athletes and other celebrities believe their agent, business manager or financial advisor is knowledgeable about exposures to their financial security and are taking steps to protect their interests. **In reality, most of these people do very little to assess and take steps to protect you from fraud and embezzlement.**

Look at a few examples of stars who suffered large, and in some cases almost total losses, who had very successful careers.

Vin Baker, Seattle Supersonics

Baker had signed a 7 year contract for $86 million in 1999 and retired in 2006. In 2012 he sued his longtime financial advisory firm for mismanaging his money and investments.

In his complaint, Baker says his financial advisor agreed to provide services "including a) management of Baker's money and investments, b) coordination of his professional advisors, accounting and financial services and c) otherwise 'manage' Baker's financial activities and condition."

The lawsuit alleges that one cause of Baker's losses was the investments he made in private businesses managed by his financial advisor – a classic conflict of interest to be avoided at all costs.

Bobby Orr, Boston Bruins

Bobby Orr is still considered by many to be the best hockey player to have played the game. He was the highest paid NHL player during his career, but thanks to his manager Alan Eagleson he ended his playing days broke. Eagleson, who was Orr's first and only manager, was also the head of the NHL Players' Association and was credited for much of the success of the first international hockey competitions between the NHL and Russian teams.

In contrast to his surface loyalty to Orr and to the game of hockey, Eagleson was later found to have defrauded Orr and other clients as well as skimmed money from the tournaments he arranged. One glaring example: just before Orr retired, he was traded to the Chicago Blackhawks. He wanted to stay in Boston but thought he hadn't gotten an offer and that the Bruins weren't interested in keeping him. Eagleson, for an unknown reason, hadn't told him that the Bruins had offered him a substantial ownership share in the team to stay. Orr, still believing he was not wanted in Boston, took an offer from Chicago that had been negotiated by Eagleson. He played only 26 games with Chicago before he retired.

Orr retired essentially broke. According to David Cruise, in his book, *Net Worth: Exploding the Myths of Pro Hockey*,

> "Eagleson, who had once said Orr was 'fixed for life', criticized Orr for 'living beyond his means' and ignoring his investment advice." [10]

As is all too common, it's very easy to blame an athlete's spending and divert attention away from the legitimate questions about how the agent or advisor handled the athlete's finances.

Orr did well after he got rid of Eagleson. Eagleson later went to prison.

Dany Heatley, Minnesota Wild

Dany Heatley filed a lawsuit against Stacey McAlpine, his former agent who became his business advisor, and supposed friend. McAlpine had helped Heatley through some very tough times after the car he was driving crashed, killing his friend and team mate Dan Snyder.

Heatley's $11 million lawsuit alleged that beginning in 2008 he invested in real estate deals with McAlpine and his family, invested in a promissory note from a related company, and allowed McAlpine access to his bank account for bill paying and investment purposes. Heatley alleges that he suffered several million dollars of investment losses and had $4 million taken from his bank account. Another NHL'er, Chris Phillips, sued McAlpine for $7.5 million over similar schemes.

McAlpine was ultimately charged criminally related to the above allegations; however he died in his sleep before the case was tried in court. Despite the civil suits and criminal charges Heatley and Phillips did not recover anything.

Sergei Fedorov, Detroit Red Wings

Sergei Fedorov was a star hockey player in Russia before he came to the U.S. and earned millions in the NHL. Unfortunately he entrusted his financial management to advisor, Joseph Zada, only to be swindled out of $43 million.

The trust between Fedorov and the advisor was reportedly so strong that Fedorov never received any paperwork documenting his investment's performance.

When the matter first went to court Zada agreed to repay Fedorov $60 million, but this was never paid. Making a bad situation even worse, Fedorov was reportedly pursued by lenders for loans taken out by his advisor but which Fedorov had unknowingly (maybe through forgery) guaranteed.

According to an article in the Detroit Free Press, Zada

"hosted extravagant parties, drove luxury cars and kept expensive homes in Grosse Pointe and Florida, according to federal documents. Zada used his victims' money to pay for his lifestyle, according to the government. (11)

An article by Andy Reid and Paula McMahon published in the Sun-Sentinel on January 22, 2016 reported that Zada was sentenced to 17 years in prison for defrauding at least 45 people over 12 years. Prosecutors said that his crimes

> "included fraudulent promissory notes, countless false statements, individuals posing as representatives of the Saudi Royal Family, actors posing as princes and princesses, international travel for purported high-level business meetings, two years of lulling victims with the assistance of numerous attorneys in Florida and Michigan, dozens upon dozens of fraudulent settlement agreements and fraudulent Saudi documents and countless fraudulent checks."

....
....

Jared Odrick et al – Avoidable Losses Case #2

Jared Odrick was one of a reported 58 investors including 30 professional athletes who invested and lost millions in promissory notes issued by Success Trade, Inc. Among the victims (besides Jared Odrick) were Victor Cruz, Brandon Knight, Joe Haden, Vernon Davis of the San Francisco 49ers; former Washington Redskins running back Clinton Portis; former Chicago Bears defensive end Adewale Ogunleye; Oakland Raiders defensive tackle Pat Sims; Minnesota Vikings defensive tackle Fred Evans; and Indiana Pacers Sam Young.

Hodge Brahmbhatt ("Brahmbhatt") had worked in the investment advisory business for several years before he started his company, Jade Private Wealth Management, LLC ("Jade") in 2008. Jade was set up to provide financial management services to professional football players. Jade was registered as a Registered Investment Adviser ("RIA") and employed Brahmbhatt as an Investment Advisor Representative ("IAR"). Brahmbhatt was also a Registered Player Financial Advisor with the NFLPA and at one time claimed to have more than 70 NFL players as clients.

Brahmbhatt worked with Fuad Ahmed at Stratton Oakmont early in his career. After Ahmed left Stratton Oakmont in 2000, he started Success Trade Securities ("STS") which was an online discount broker-dealer. In 2009, in addition to his role at Jade, Brahmbhatt became an employee and Registered Representative of STS.

According to FINRA, Jade's investment managers (including Brahmbhatt) recommended athletes invest through STS. STS sold the players Promissory Notes that had interest rates of up to 26% for three years. When they became due, many clients were convinced to roll over their investment into new Promissory Notes and some others were convinced to convert the notes to shares of STI. They were told that STI was going to become a public company and would be worth significantly more in a short time.

Unknown to investors, STS was alleged to have paid at least $1.25 million to Jade, presumably for referring clients who invested in the promissory notes.

Issues:

Brahmbhatt was a NFLPA Registered Player Financial Advisor but this provides no assurance to players that the advisor is honest or competent.

Brahmbhatt had a severe undisclosed conflict of interest – he was a Registered Representative of STS and was receiving money from STS for finding investors.

STS and STI were both in very poor financial condition and could not have continued to operate without receiving money from new investors.

Jade was also in very poor financial condition and relied upon new investor money, in the form of commissions and loans from STS, to continue to operate.

Investors paid their money to STS or STI where it was completely under the control of Ahmed.

There was no independent custodian to hold the investments and actually receive interest payments when due, or report if the interest was not received.

The Promissory Notes were simply promises to pay the money back. If STI couldn't pay the interest or pay back the principal, there was no security or other source of money to pay back the investors.

Fuad lied about future events that he said would make shares of STI a good investment, but these were not checked out.

Investors did little to no due diligence on STS or STI since they trusted their advisor, believing he had performed due diligence and also because the investment was recommended by other athletes.

Avoidable Losses?

A search on Brokercheck would have identified that Brahmbhatt had prior complaints against him and that he was a Registered Representative of STS. This conflict of interest should have been disclosed to his clients but was not. An investor discovering the conflict should immediately drop any idea of following his advice or continuing to use him as an advisor.

Brahmbhatt and Ahmed had both been employed at Stratton Oakmont which was expelled from the investment industry in 1999. Stratton Oakmont is best known for its boiler room operation which was portrayed in the movie, *Wolf of Wall Street*, where salespeople manipulated and pressured people to invest in worthless stocks. An advisor who stays for more than a few weeks with a firm like Stratton Oakmont is probably not of the highest ethical standards and represents a very risky choice for you.

The high interest rates on the promissory notes should have been a red flag. High rates mean high risk and why would they offer such high rates unless they couldn't get money elsewhere? If an institution in the business of lending money won't lend them money, why should you?

Promissory Notes are very risky since you are passing over your money with no security and no transparency. You have no ability to see what is actually done with the money.

STS and STI's finances were in bad shape. A request for financial statements and a credit check would have shown that they were only able to operate because of new investor money, and they certainly weren't going to be able to pay the additional large amounts of interest they owed on the Notes. If they refused to provide the requested information then it's an easy decision to walk away.

Ahmed's story that STI would soon become a publicly traded company would quickly have been discredited if documented details had been requested and followed up on.

In short, even basic due diligence would have identified red flags exposing the fact that this was a very risky investment. Digging a little deeper would have disclosed that it just wasn't a legitimate investment with any chance of earning the stated interest rate and returning your capital.

. . . .
. . . .

Summary

Hopefully the brief run through of issues above has illustrated that the investing environment is very risky and full of conflicts of interest or worse, especially for those who aren't familiar with this world. A few key points to remember include:

Trust is not your friend when it comes to your money. Fraudsters will work very hard to gain your trust because that leads to opportunities for them to gain access to your money.

Your first step needs to be to accept that trust is a big risk with potentially big negative consequences. With that mindset you will begin to be able to recognize the manipulation tactics and red flags discussed in this book for what they really are.

> *"The main thing about money, Bud, is that it makes you do things you don't want to do."*
>
> – Lou Mannheim (Hal Holbrook) "*Wall Street*" 1987

This isn't a do it yourself investment guide. It isn't intended to cover all the information you should have to manage your own investments. You will likely need good professional help to get things done properly, and as the saying goes: **if you think good advice is too expensive, wait until you find out how much bad or crooked advice will cost you.**

Before jumping into the discussion about advisors, try this true or false quiz.

1. Having your investment advisor also look after your accounting and taxes is riskier than having separate firms do them.
2. It is quite normal for your advisor to receive a portion of the profits you make on your investments.
3. All financial advisors and advisory firms have to carry insurance that will protect you if your advisor did steal from you.
4. It is a financial advisor's responsibility to ensure you don't become a fraud victim.
5. Industry or company awards are given to top brokers based on producing exceptional results for their clients.
6. Financial advisors who are quoted by magazines or have radio shows on investing or managing money are well qualified or they wouldn't be offered those opportunities.
7. An advisor asking you to pay your investment money directly to him is a big problem.
8. If your financial advisor summarizes your bank and investment account statements for you, it is okay if you don't get statements directly from the bank and investment custodian or review the activity in your account.

Answers

1. True. Many frauds have occurred when one advisor or firm is looking after all of your finances including your accounting. Having your investment advisor also look after your accounting and taxes is riskier than having separate firms do them.
2. False – Only under certain circumstances is an advisor allowed to share in the profits made on your investments. If you qualify as an accredited investor, it may be acceptable but why agree to it? I doubt he would also be agreeing to cover part of any losses you might suffer.
3. False - All financial advisors and advisory firms do not have to carry insurance that will protect you if your advisor did steal from you. If they do carry insurance, it is important to know what types of losses would be covered and for how much.
4. False – Although many people may think that their financial advisor will just naturally do the things that need to be done to protect you from fraud, very few actually do. They often fall short in the areas discussed in this book as do many investors.
5. False - Company awards are given to top earning advisors and are not based on the returns earned by their clients. They really reward the best sales people. Industry awards are also not dependent on their clients' returns but based on non-investment criteria. Some even require payment by the advisor or firm to be considered or to buy advertising.
6. False - Financial advisors wanting to establish credibility have numerous public routes to follow. Being quoted in magazines or having radio shows gives them good exposure. While some are undoubtedly competent and doing this as a way to help people, many others offer only self-serving advice that is not in your best interest. A search on the words "financial advisor radio show host fraud" just now returned 765,000 results. Clearly those includes many duplicates but just looking at the first page of results gives

more than a dozen separate examples of advisors with radio shows being charged with fraud. Being quoted by a magazine isn't necessarily a bad thing but don't think it is a substitute for proper diligence on the advisor.

7. True - An investment advisor asking you to hand over the money for an investment directly to him is a big problem. It isn't a normal request and leaves you at risk of having the money stolen. Your money should be paid to your investment or brokerage account or to the company you are investing in.

8. False - If your financial advisor summarizes your investment account statements for you, you still want to be sure to get your account statements directly from the investment custodian or go online directly into your account to review the activity. Having your advisor receive account statements directly and providing you only a summary would allow the summaries to be fabricated and any missing funds or other problems to be covered up indefinitely.

If you got these all correct, congratulations! But there's more to consider.

Conflicts of Interest

> *"It's all about bucks, kid. The rest is conversation. "*
> – Gordon Gekko (Michael Douglas) – "*Wall Street*" 1987

When investing, your objective is to earn a return that is reasonable in relation to the amount of risk involved. The advisor's interest is to make money off you by charging you fees or receiving commissions for selling you the investment products. Your interest and the advisor's interest will be in conflict if, for example, the investment that is best for you pays him the least. If his objective is to make the most money for him, but the best investments for you pay him less than other not so good investments, there is a conflict of interest.

Clearly if your advisor's goal is to make as much money off of you as he can, you aren't going to get the best investment advice.

Fiduciary Duty or Suitability: Who's Interest Comes First?

If someone owes you a fiduciary duty under the law they have to put your interests ahead of their own. Most people would expect that someone they are trusting with their money to give them investment advice would put their best interests first, but that's clearly not always the case.

If the salesperson/advisor is a Registered Representative employed by a broker-dealer he may not have to put your interest first when recommending what to invest in. They may even owe a fiduciary duty to their employer, meaning they are expected to put your interest second to the firm's.

Generally, Registered Representatives only have to recommend a product that is suitable for you. Something can be argued to be suitable even if it costs you more than investing in essentially the same product from a different company.

On the other hand, Investment Advisor Representatives ("IAR's"), who work for Registered Investment Advisers ("RIA") have a fiduciary duty to put your interests ahead of their own when advising you on what to invest in.

A third category of people who may approach you with investment opportunities are called Promoters. Promoters are not advisors; they are sales people and possibly con-men. They do not have a fiduciary duty to you. You should expect that they are putting their own interest far ahead of yours. Don't think they are advising you, rather you should assume they are trying to get you to invest in their product or business without any concern for the impact it may have on you.

It is critical to understand whether your advisor has and will acknowledge in writing that he has a fiduciary duty to you in all his services to you. If he won't, you should find another advisor. If he does, that doesn't mean he should automatically be hired.

An acknowledgement of a fiduciary duty to you, in writing, is a starting point in determining whether you will work with a particular advisor, but it is far from the only consideration.

Advisor's Compensation Matters

I think everyone realizes that people respond to financial incentives. That's why athletes' contracts so often include bonuses for achieving performance targets: batting average, number of sacks, points per game, goals and assists.

If your advisor gets paid commissions based on the investments you buy, a conflict of interests exists. Since some investments pay higher commissions, it's natural that advisors would be more motivated to sell these.

It's also quite possible that the person recommending the investment products doesn't really understand which investment is best for you. There is minimal (if any) training provided by broker-dealers to their Registered Representatives on the products they are paid to sell. They may not realize that the products they are selling are very complex and only suitable for a small number of people with specific needs. Consider this:

> "We're surprised at how many (registered) reps cannot explain the products they sell," said Tanya Solov, Illinois securities director. [5]

If your advisor doesn't understand the investment products, it's even more likely his commission will be the deciding factor in their recommendation to you. After all, if he believes both products are good for you, why not recommend the one that pays him the most? Of course they aren't likely to actually be equally good for you.

It's important, then, to understand how the person advising you is paid. If incentives like higher commissions didn't work to get salespeople to sell those investments, all investment products would logically pay sales people the same commissions.

You can reduce the likelihood of a conflict of interest created by commissions by dealing with an advisor who is paid by "fee only". In other words, they don't get paid commissions; they are paid by you based on an hourly fee, a fixed fee or fee based on a percent of your investments.

If you don't have a fee only advisor, make sure that any time a product is recommended you find out their commission on the product recommended, what other products they considered for you, and why they recommended this product.

Even with a fee only advisor caution is needed. Some advisors who call themselves "fee only" advisors are not telling the whole story and they may earn commissions on some products. Make sure you understand what the person claiming to be a "fee only" advisor means by that.

Other Conflicts

Besides commissions, what are some examples of other conflicts an advisor might have?

In connection with investment recommendations, conflicts can include:

- If your advisor has invested in the same **private** investment he is recommending to you, this is also a potential conflict, even if he lets you know. Consider this: how would you know if he was more interested in helping raise money to support his own investment or in finding you the best investment opportunity? If the advisor has a stake in the business, he likely needs the money either to complete or continue development or operation. His potential benefit from your investment could motivate him to recommend it whether it is the best use of your money or not.
- Advisors having sales quotas of certain investments that they must sell to earn a bonus;
- Broker-dealers also own investments they bought for the purpose of reselling at some point. When they want to get

rid of some investment they own, they offer incentives to their Registered Representatives to sell those shares;

- Proprietary investment products are investments that are created or "manufactured" by broker-dealers (as opposed to having been manufactured by some other company and sold by the broker-dealer). Proprietary products have a higher profit for the broker-dealer and so Registered Representatives can be incented or pressured to sell these. The higher profit to the broker-dealer will mean a higher cost and/or higher expenses for you;

- Other investment product "manufacturers" or fund managers will sometimes invite advisors out to very high end events, golf courses, sporting events, etc. at their expense. If the advisor enjoys these sorts of outings and hopes to be invited again, they need to sell some of that manufacturer's investment products. If they then recommend that product to you, is it in your best interest or is it influenced by the treatment they have received?

- Advisors may also have undisclosed side arrangements whereby they are paid by the product manufacturer or asset manager for selling or placing investors in certain investments. These are essentially kickbacks. If they are disclosed they might be called referral fees but they still represent a conflict of interest and you should steer clear.

A Team Game

It is clear from the publicly reported cases of major financial losses suffered by athletes and celebrities that in many cases an advisor, agent or business manager has been involved in creating the risk that led to the loss or missed the risk. Either way, your advisors represent a considerable risk to your wealth if you don't have the right team, processes, and controls. Too often, advisors have been selected solely on the advice of another player or friend. Don't fall into that trap. Ensure you really know who you are choosing.

The starting point, and the decision that will likely make a huge difference to your financial security, is the selection of your advisory team.

The following list consists of common services you may use at some point:

- Financial planning
- Budgeting
- Estate planning
- Asset protection planning
- Cash management
- Business management
- Negotiating contracts
- Collecting and depositing your earnings
- Bill paying and/or check signing
- Withdrawing cash for you
- Transfering money
- Arranging loans for you
- Recommending, buying, selling and managing investments
- Arranging travel
- Arranging insurance
- Hiring household or other staff
- Accounting and record keeping
- Providing financial reports
- Preparing your taxes

An important question to consider is whether you want one firm to do everything for you.

The answer is no.

Having one person or one firm handle all or most of the above services increases your risk of financial loss significantly. The reason for that is if one person/firm has control over your money and can record and report how it is being used or invested without anyone independent seeing what is really happening, they can mismanage or steal your money and falsify the records to hide it.

There are three principles that you should absolutely follow in assembling your team:

1. Do not let one person or firm have control over all of your financial affairs. Any person or firm that has access to your bank accounts, investments or other assets should not be doing your accounting i.e. keeping records of what is happening with your money, investments and other assets.
2. Have the contract(s) with your advisor(s) state in writing exactly which services your advisor is responsible for providing, and how you will be charged, and don't assume they are doing anything more.
3. Do not let any person or firm handle any of your bank accounts, investments, income collection or expense payments without independent oversight. The oversight should be performed by you if you do have an understanding of the risks or by a financially knowledgeable representative of your choice who has the following: 1.) No connections to your advisors or their firms, 2.) No conflicts of interest, and 3.) No access to or control over your money or investments. (Access can be obtained in many ways and is discussed later.)

To protect yourself, having a team of advisors allows you to separate the people who have access to your wealth from those who record the transactions and prepare reports on them. Preferably have separate, independent parties doing the following:

- Negotiate your contracts,
- Provide financial and investment advice and management,
- Do your accounting and prepare your taxes, and
- Provide legal advice.

The titles of the people or firms providing financial and investment advice and management can be confusing and are not consistent. They may be called investments advisors, financial advisors, financial managers, business managers, personal managers, wealth managers or something else entirely. It's not so important what they are called as what they do for you and what access they have to your money and investments. It's particularly important that the accounting function is independent of those who provide financial advice or management.

Remember also that **an agent or financial or investment advisory firm that also has a division or related company to do your accounting does not qualify as independent.**

Although they are not advisors, certain other functions should also be separated. If you use a bill pay firm to pay your bills it should not be the same firm doing your accounting. Likewise, the Custodian who holds your investments should be independent from your other advisors.

Ideally you want your advisors to be independent of each other but to work cooperatively and coordinate the management of your financial affairs.

Working with Your Financial Advisors

The extent to which your financial advisors have access to or control over your money and investments is something that should be limited as much as possible. Some firms will want access to or control over all your accounts, arguing they need the flexibility to make decisions and take advantage of opportunities in your best interests, or to relieve you of having to spend time or be involved.

In contrast, you can have an advisor who has no access to or control over your accounts. Under this type of arrangement, you could open your own investment account at a brokerage firm where you have access online to purchase or sell investments. Your advisor could still provide input or direction to you but you could be the only one with access to your accounts and authority to make transactions or transfers.

Between these two positions, you can arrange your accounts so that your advisor has limited access to certain accounts but not others, and limit the transactions in those accounts.

For certain, one thing you want to have in place is an independent custodian to hold your investments, record your ownership, collect interest and dividends and send reports of your holdings and activity directly to you. The largest known investment fraud was perpetrated by Bernie Madoff. He was able to pull this off for many years because there was no independent custodian holding the clients' investments. He sent out statements to clients showing that he was making investments and earning great returns for them; but in fact he wasn't making any investments with their money. Having an independent custodian hold your investments is a must.

Contracts

It is quite likely that the terms of the contract you sign with your agent will be dictated by the league.

Regardless of whether it is your agent or another advisor or business manager who is providing you with financial advice or services, you should insist on having a written contract specific to the financial services being provided to you. This isn't legal advice; it's business advice.

Your contracts with all of your financial advisors should –

1. State exactly what services will be provided.
2. State exactly how you will be charged, how it will be calculated and how it will be paid.
3. Specify what expenses, if any, will be charged to you.
4. If your earnings are being deposited with your advisors (which I strongly believe is a mistake), require that all of your funds be deposited directly into a bank account in your name and not be co-mingled with funds belonging to other clients or the advisor or firm.
5. For bill pay services, require that electronic copies of all invoices, bills, etc. that are paid are provided to you, or a designated party, and reviewed monthly.
6. Include a Right to Audit Clause allowing you to have a representative examine all records necessary to audit

compliance with the contract and correctness of all aspects of the handling of your affairs, including transactions and accounting.

7. Be reviewed by your attorney before signing.

The Importance of Your Advisor's Character

Character encompasses many elements including: integrity, ethics, fairness, motivation, commitment, respect, self-discipline, tolerance, reliability, loyalty, and compassion. It's the inner guide that shapes who you are; what you do when no-one is looking and no-one will know.

Trusting your career and future to someone without good character is asking for problems, whether they are handling your finances or not. They will create problems when you least need them.

Unfortunately, you can only see someone's character through their actions.

Some agents have a reputation for being willing to do whatever it takes, ethical or not, to get their deal. This may sound like the type who will get you the best contract, the highest salary, the biggest bonuses. Unfortunately, in some cases the "whatever it takes" can mean going so far as to leave a client without a deal at all if the deal won't enhance their own reputation.

So what do your dealings with your advisors tell you? If they are publicity seeking, self-promoting and self-centered, that isn't what you need. This type will tell you everything you want to hear but, in reality, they put themselves before you.

Think about how the advisor has dealt with you so far and what that tells you about his character. Consider the following:

- Before you turned pro, did they abide by the NCAA recruiting rules or have they tried to use money, gifts, cars, etc. to lure you? Perhaps a job for a family member? If they are willing to cheat for you, how can you be sure they won't cheat you next time?

- If they offered you money or gifts, were they doing it to help you or them? They want you as a client so they can make money off you. They are manipulating you and, if you're still playing under NCAA rules, your career is being put at risk. Why would they do this if they were truly looking out for you?
- Do they share confidential information about other clients to impress you? Would you want your information shared with others? Not only is that putting his interests first, it can also be putting your wealth at risk. With the prevalence of identity theft today, you don't want anyone giving out your private information, financial or otherwise, to anyone.
- Have they focused on what's best for you, not just how much money they can get you? Getting you the most money also gets them the most money, but will they work to get you something you really want if it means less money (for them)? Plus, what's the point of getting a contract for the most dollars possible if your money is just going to be mismanaged or otherwise lost?
- If an agent wants to manage your finances, has he pressured you to use their firm for financial management? Has he made that a condition?
- Does he/she openly discuss the fees and the expenses you will be charged? If not, ask for specifics. If they are reluctant to discuss fees, it's not a good sign.

If your prospective advisors aren't playing it straight, chances are they really see you just for the money they can make.

> "What we have found is that if a guy will cheat to get you, he will cheat you when he gets you," NFL Players Association President Trace Armstrong said. [12]

- Do they show an interest in more than just the size of your contract? For instance,
    - Have they spent time trying to understand what is important to you, what your goals are, what you aspire to after playing?

- Do they talk about needing to be careful with your finances and building a financial plan that will protect and grow your wealth?
- Do they try to educate you about financial management?
- Do they encourage, and demonstrate in their actions, financial responsibility?

If not, then they are more interested in their financial welfare than yours.

....
....

Tim Duncan – Avoidable Losses Case #3

A lawsuit filed by Tim Duncan claims he was defrauded of $20 million by Charles Banks. Apparently, Duncan started working with Charles Banks in 1998 when Banks was President of CSI Capital Management (CSI). Duncan became a client of CSI for tax planning, tax compliance, financial advisory services and also for investment counseling. A couple of years later CSI began managing Duncan's day to day finances.

An article in the Chicago Tribune in 2000 quoted Banks on one of the financial problems college athletes faced.

> "In retrospect, those were the good old days. Today's athlete has to beware not only of the sleazy so called street agent brokering deals for the sleazy so-called agent waiting to sign him, but of a whole slew of smooth talkers who like to call themselves financial planners.
>
> "It's one of the biggest abuses in college sports right now," said **Charles Banks, a legitimate financial advisor for a San Francisco firm that handles as many Fortune 500 CEOs and entertainers as pro athletes."** [13]

In 2015 Duncan filed a lawsuit claiming that Banks steered him into investments in which Banks had a personal interest and caused him losses. In addition, Banks allegedly arranged for

Duncan to make a loan to Gameday Entertainment, LLC in 2012 for $7,500,000. Subsequently Comerica Bank also claimed that Duncan guaranteed a $6,000,000 loan it made to Gameday but Duncan claims his signature was forged.

Issues

An article entitled "NBA star Tim Duncan says losses from financial advisor topped $20 million" in Investment News, quoted Duncan as saying,

> 'I thought, for the most part, I was keeping an eye on things. You have to have people checking on people checking on people. I did that for a while. Obviously, I got to a point where the people I trusted were checking on themselves," said Mr. Duncan." [14]

It is alleged that most of Duncan's money was invested in companies in which Banks and/or CSI had an ownership interest or performed a management function.

As in so many cases, Duncan was relying on related firms to provide most, if not all, the financial services he required. This is always a dangerous proposition.

Avoidable Losses?

Clearly, simply dealing with someone for a long period of time does not mean you are safe from fraud; nor does the credibility that supposedly comes from being quoted in the press. When an investment is being recommended to you, you need to understand why it is being recommended and whether your advisor has any conflicts. If appropriate background research (due diligence) had been performed on the investments, the alleged conflict of interest would likely have been identified. At that point the relationship with Banks and CSI should have been terminated.

Although it is not possible to stop someone from forging your signature, you should insist on always obtaining copies of documents that you have signed. Further, you should insist on receiving monthly personal financial statements that include a listing of all investment purchases and sales in the month along with any agreements, contracts or other legal documents that pertain to you or your financial affairs.

Finally, you, or an independent representative, should always be monitoring your accounts, investments and other areas of risk.

....
....

Choosing the Right Financial Advisors

> **"Getting an unsophisticated client was the golden prize. The quickest way to make money on Wall Street is to take the most sophisticated product and try to sell it to the least sophisticated client."**
>
> - **Greg Smith, October 21, 2012 on *60 Minutes, cbsnews.com, "Goldman Sachs VP explains why he quit"***

Pension plans with billions of dollars to invest have very qualified management, but they still hire independent advisory firms to help them evaluate investment managers before passing over the first dollar. Why would they pay for help picking investment advisors?

The biggest reason is because once you have passed over your money, if you passed it over to a crook, you likely won't ever get it back.

There are two very common scenarios associated with big losses:

1. Countless numbers of embezzlement schemes and investment frauds have started when a trusted advisor suffered a financial setback. Until the setback they had been operating honestly, but in an effort to preserve their reputation and their clients, they hid the losses and borrowed from client accounts, intending to make back the losses. However, when they suffered more losses and their financial situation became worse, it became easier each time to

continue taking client funds. In other words, advisors, like any other people, are often honest until some financial pressure leads them to act dishonestly. Once it has happened, it's a slippery slope, and with each bad choice it becomes easier for that person to continue stealing your future financial security.

A variation of the above scenario that seems to happen more in the sports world occurs when the advisor starts living the lifestyle of his clients, but doesn't really have the income to pay for it. Perhaps it's a feeling of having to keep up appearances or perhaps it's just greed; enjoying the celebrity life so much they choose to use clients' money rather than live more modestly and honestly.

2. The second scenario involves what are essentially career criminals, who are often sociopaths. They will seem genuinely interested in your good fortune and will be very convincing in their explanation of why they are making this great opportunity is available to you. But no matter how convincing they seem remember, if you believe what you hear is true, **verify** the information and investment before considering passing over your money. If they say they need an answer now or tell you that you can't discuss the opportunity with anyone, walk away no matter how good it sounds.

The best con men are very convincing. They will talk their way around your questions or concerns without really answering them. They will avoid providing proof of what they tell you. They will describe exactly what you want to hear and make it sound like they are doing you a favor by taking your money. But an experienced, knowledgeable, independent consultant will have a much greater chance of seeing through the façade, if that's what it is.

You might want to consider using a consultant to find and pre-qualify two or three competent advisors for you to interview. This way, the interviews are your chance to figure out if you could work with someone, already knowing that they are well qualified. **Then your interview isn't about you assessing their capabilities; rather it's about comfort, his/her focus on your needs, and how he/she would work with you.**

You may think that using a consultant to pre-qualify advisors is overkill, especially considering that you can go on the internet and find lists of questions to ask an advisor you are considering working with. The problem is that if you don't know exactly what the question is trying to evaluate, or what the answers should be, or what problems certain answers might indicate, asking those questions is of little value. If the advisor isn't honest, he will be able to convince you that either the answer doesn't matter or will answer with the appropriate answer, whether it's true or not.

As a forensic accountant with 30 years' experience conducting fraud examinations, I know that one of the keys when interviewing someone you are evaluating is to ask questions that (1) you already know the answer to or (2) will provide meaningful information that you can later research and verify. Either way, you are finding out about their integrity. Unfortunately, it's difficult for inexperienced investors to be able to accurately evaluate the integrity or competence of a potential advisor.

Whether the potential advisor asks you questions is also important. You have a right to expect that you will receive advice customized to your unique situation. If the advisor doesn't ask questions about you, your background, family, goals, plans, priorities and other questions, and spend time getting to know you and what you need, he isn't the right choice. Find someone else.

Hedge Fund Boss Preying on African-Americans Arrested

"Two things are infinite: the universe and human stupidity; and I'm not sure about the universe."

"Those were the words that Fredrick Douglas Scott attached to most of the emails sent to the clients of his boutique investment banking and financial advisory firm, ACI Capital. What the clients didn't realize was that the joke was on them, according to federal prosecutors.

In addition to being one of *Ebony* magazine's "Top 30 under 30" and claiming to be the youngest African-American to found a hedge fund, Fredrick Douglas Scott was a fraudster, according to the criminal complaint filed Monday in U.S. District Court for the Eastern District of New York. The complaint was unsealed Tuesday after Scott was arrested." [15]

As with so many advisors who defraud their clients, Scott had fooled a lot of people along the way, including investors and other very smart people. It takes knowledge and diligence to see through the false face of an accomplished fraudster.

It's a Business Arrangement

Always remember that your relationship and interaction with your advisor is a business arrangement. The goal of the arrangement is to help you meet your long term financial goals and have a secure financial future. You are paying your advisor and have a right to expect that everything in the arrangement is being done in your best interest. You always have the right to know what is being done with your assets and to get an independent second opinion. You don't owe your advisor your blind trust, just the fees you have agreed to pay for legitimate services.

If you're just looking for a friend, get a dog, not an advisor.

Due Diligence – Evaluating an Advisor

I have read a good deal of advice from industry insiders about how to select your advisors.

Some have said ask a family member or friend who they have used and whether they have been satisfied.

Others have said make sure you pick someone whose personality you connect with.

I have no problem with saying that a personal connection is a good thing to consider, but only **after** making sure first that they are honest and qualified in all other respects.

Other advice I have heard is to choose the advisor who is obviously the most successful, but what is success in the financial industry? Generally, awards are given to advisors who earn the most money for their employers; it doesn't have anything to do with how much his clients make on their portfolios.

There is no chance you will recognize a fraudster by whether you connect with them or not. The biggest frauds have been committed by people who understand human nature and have learned how to manipulate their victims. Chances are that the better fraudsters are going to make you feel at ease. They want you to feel comfortable with them, ultimately to get your trust.

Don't select your advisor based on some connection you share unless you have first done thorough research. Good con artists will always establish some connection with you; they find out you have two kids, they tell you they also have two; you played football, they played football; you go to church, so do they. It gives them something supposedly in common with you, a starting point to get you to relax your doubts or skepticism.

People hoping to gain an advantage will try to take this connection with you further, by professing a commitment to a church or a special purpose or group you support. This is also known as an "affinity" and is often used to enable fraud.

Affinity fraud is a term describing a situation where a scam artist preys on people who are members of the same affinity group. One of the favorite affinities used for fraudulent purposes is membership in the same church. People sharing the same faith are more likely to trust each other, and this is used against you.

The point is that **having a connection or affinity doesn't mean that the advisor is competent or honest.** You, or someone acting on your behalf, have to perform due diligence and verify the advisor's background through independent sources, no matter how comfortable you feel with them. This is true even if you have known the person a long time. You only get to know the part of a fraudster that they want you to see.

According to an article in Investment News [16], about 12% of registered securities professionals have some type of disclosure event on their records. A disclosure event is not a good sign. It's likely a customer complaint or regulatory action. And it's easy to check out through Brokercheck, a website operated by FINRA, but very few people bother.

There is a considerable amount of information about advisors and advisory firms available online if you look in the right places (and understand what it means).

Hedge Fund Manager Pleads Guilty in $2.6 Million Ponzi Scheme

U.S. Attorney's Office, Southern District of California

July 16, 2015

"According to his plea agreement in the criminal case, Moore established Coast Capital Management LLC in 2009, when he began soliciting friends and acquaintances to invest in this "hedge fund." Moore told two investors that he had earned an undergraduate degree in economics from a respected state university, had worked as a senior analyst at a large, national securities firm, had registered himself and his firm with securities regulators, and was making tremendous profits for his clients through his knowledge and expertise in securities trading."

This should have been an easy scheme to avoid, given the things he was saying to investors. They could have found out that he didn't have a degree, hadn't worked at the securities firm, and neither he nor his firm were registered with FINRA or the SEC. None of these statements would have required a great deal of work to determine that they were not true.

Is Being Registered by the Players Association Enough?

The NFLPA established the Financial Advisors Program in 2002 offering certification of financial advisors who meet certain criteria and pay a fee. The NBPA and NHLPA don't offer any similar programs or certification. The MLBPA offers a Limited Certification as a Player Agent for people who provide financial advice or services to players in affiliation with a Player Agent. Financial advisors who are not affiliated with a Player Agent can't receive MLBPA but this does not prevent them from providing financial advice or services the MLB players.

The NFLPA Financial Advisors Program certifies financial advisors who want to provide services to players and who meet certain criteria. Similar to the MLB Limited Certification program, lack of certification by the Financial Advisors Program does not preclude financial advisors from providing services to NFL players.

To be absolutely clear, registration of your financial advisor in the Registered Financial Advisors Program does not provide any assurance that these people are honest or competent; and the NFLPA is not taking responsibility for fraud or embezzlement or incompetence by registered advisors. The NFLPA site states that, "no individual financial advisor or company will be recommended over any other, nor will any specific advisor or firm be marketed to players by the NFLPA." Further, it states that Registered Financial Advisors are "not permitted to state or imply that NFLPA registration constitutes an endorsement and/or recommendation by the NFLPA of you or your services, or that your registration status constitutes evidence of your skill, honesty or competence to represent players." Unfortunately, it seems to be widely believed that the certified financial advisors can be counted on to be honest and competent. This has the unintended consequence of giving the advisor credibility and lowering a player's caution.

In order to register with the NFLPA a financial advisor is subject to a background check and must have certain qualifications, which are not particularly difficult. **But after registration there is**

no ongoing oversight of the advisors by the NFLPA. This is a serious weakness and puts the players at risk. A background check, even when done thoroughly, only covers the advisor's past. It does not mean someone will never be dishonest and it doesn't prevent someone from committing a dishonest act in the future.

As will be discussed below, **you absolutely must perform your own due diligence on your advisors or have an independent knowledgeable party perform it on your behalf.** Certification is very narrowly focused. It does not reduce the need to do your own research.

Should You Follow the Stars?

Large agencies often end up representing many of the A-list stars in all the major sports. As large agencies, they generally provide complete management including finding their clients other income opportunities and providing financial management. From the outside, it may appear that if so many stars go to these agencies, they must be the most desirable for all players. But that's not always true.

First, the bigger agencies are all about business, and making money off their stable of athletes is paramount. They offer the full spectrum of services but they can be costly (profitable for them). As a result, they make more money off their stars and accordingly pay most of their attention to them. This is fine if you are a star, but if you are not in this group, you may find yourself getting little attention, especially when it comes to promoting you. These agencies will probably always be happy to provide accounting and investment services (for their fees) but you likely won't receive the same representation as the A-list. You may be better off with a smaller agency that will have the time and interest to promote you.

Does Your Advisor Acknowledge a Fiduciary Duty to You?

As mentioned earlier, in selecting your advisor, one of the first things you should be concerned about is whether your advisor acknowledges a fiduciary duty to you. Having a fiduciary duty to you means that your advisor must legally put your interests ahead of all others, including his own. This would seem to be an obvious expectation of someone you are paying to advise you what to do with your money or investments, but it can't be taken for granted.

Take note, although acknowledgement by the advisor of a fiduciary duty to you should be a requirement, it should not be taken as a guarantee that they will always live up to that duty. Many fraudsters have found it easy to say they are a fiduciary when it is actually just part of their scam.

Regulatory Research – Does Your Advisor Have a Clean Record?

RIA's, their Investment Adviser Representatives must be registered with either the SEC or the state securities regulator. Broker-dealers must register with the SEC but individual registered representatives must register with FINRA, pass a qualifying examination, and be licensed by the state securities regulator. You can find regulatory information on them starting at FINRA's Broker-Check (http://brokercheck.finra.org/Search/Search.aspx).

Information available from Broker-Check includes

- Whether an advisor or firm is registered;
- Information that has been disclosed to the regulator including regulatory actions, criminal convictions, and in some cases, complaints; and
- The advisor's qualifications and employment history.

Another case illustrates how a few minutes on Broker-Check would have saved investors a lot of grief and lost money. In 2015 the SEC filed a Complaint against Scott Valente and his firm ELIV Group, LLC which described his scheme as follows:

Scott Valente and his firm ELIV Group, LLC "fraudulently solicited those investments by: (1) falsely claiming to prospective clients that ELIV achieved consistent and outsized, positive returns; (2) falsely assuring prospective clients that their principal was "guaranteed," backed by a large money market fund and fully liquid; (3) sending clients false monthly investment reports that reported inflated monthly returns, account values and assets under management; (4) falsely assuring prospective and existing clients that ELIV's books and records (including monthly statements) were audited; and (5) falsely misrepresenting that ELIV was qualified to and would open and manage IRA accounts for its clients." Scott Valente was also found guilty of criminal charges and was sentenced to 20 years in prison, and ordered to pay about $8.2 million in restitution).

Scott Valente's regulatory record on Broker-Check shows that his registration had been terminated by FINRA in 2009, and before that his record showed more than 20 complaints during his 20 years as a stockbroker. Most of the complaints were settled with payments to the client or were found in the client's favor resulting in an award to the client. Complaints involved allegations of unauthorized trades in their accounts or sale of unsuitable investments. If his clients had been aware of the Broker-Check information, there would have been little chance they would have passed over their money to someone so obviously untrustworthy.

Not all people who say they are investment advisors are registered. If an investment advisor is not registered or exempt from registration, you should not deal with them.

The second place to check is the Investment Advisers Public Disclosure website at http://www.adviserinfo.sec.gov/IAPD/default.aspx . This contains information about Registered Investment Adviser firms and Investment Adviser Representatives.

Competence and Credentials/Designations

No matter how friendly or trustworthy an advisor is, you don't want him handling your financial affairs or making investments for you if he isn't competent. But, believe me, even an incompetent advisor can sound very competent if you aren't familiar with the investments he is talking about.

If you are doing the due diligence on an advisor yourself, you should find out what certifications or designations he/she has. Some certifications require much more extensive training, comprehensive examinations and ongoing education; others require very little. All else being equal, you would expect that more extensive training should lead to greater competence.

You should also be aware that some advisors claim certifications that are simply made up. If you come across this, it will tell you all you need to know about his/her incompetence and lack of integrity.

Credentials that are widely acknowledged as credible evidence of competence include the following:

- CFP – Certified Financial Planner
- CPA – Certified Public Accountant
- FPS – Financial Planning Specialist
- CFA – Chartered Financial Analyst

You can look up information on many additional professional designations at www.finra.org/Investors/ToolsCalculators/ProfessionalDesignations/DesignationsLookup/ .

This site will provide information about many designations, including their requirements and how much ongoing education is required. You can check their status directly with most reputable organizations.

Reputation

Reputation should also be investigated. Talking to people who have dealt with the advisor is a good start. How well do they know him? How long did they work with him? What kind of experience did they have while working with him and after? What concerns did they have? Would they work with him again?

This isn't just a matter of asking people how they like him. It should be a deep dive; talking to clients, inquiring into complaints, looking for lawsuits, reading online references, talking to former employees, asking about awards received, and who he associates with.

Financial Advisor Fees

You should be concerned about an advisor who avoids clearly explaining the fees you will be charged.   You are entitled to know what you will be paying.

As mentioned earlier, investment advisors can charge in different ways, including:

- Commissions charged on investments purchased;
- A fee based on a percentage of your assets under management ("AUM") which is essentially your investments. This fee might range from half a percent of the value of your investments up to two and a half percent. Anything over 1% is too high.
- An hourly fee;
- A fixed fee; or
- A combination of the above.

If you are an Accredited Investor, your investment advisor may be allowed to charge you a fee plus part of the profits you make on your investments. Although this might sound like a way of aligning his interests with yours, it also may have the unwanted effect of having him select very risky investments in the hope of a big win; and nothing to lose if it's a big loss instead.

As discussed above, a fee only advisor might also collect commissions on the products you invest in. If so, this must be disclosed to you; but even if disclosed, this can put your best interests in conflict with theirs.

Commission rates are not standard from firm to firm. Further, they are negotiable and for certain products commissions on purchases over a certain $ amount are lowered. You should be told these things.

Some advisors will offset the commissions they receive against their normal fee, thereby removing the conflict of interest.

Make sure that if they say this, it is included in your contract with the advisor and is reflected in the calculations of fees you are charged.

Business Managers, financial advisors and others providing non-investment services basically charge whatever the client agrees to. The fees should be spelled out clearly in the Advisory Agreement including how many dollars the services will cost you. You should get a second estimate from another firm that offers the same service to ensure you are not being ripped off.

Should You Choose a Big or Small Firm?

Whether you choose to work with an advisor from a large Wall Street firm or a small RIA, you can't take for granted that your money and investments will be properly invested and safeguarded. For example, an article in The National Law Review by Brian Mahany dated January 28, 2015 entitled *UBS Financial Services Accused of Trust Fraud* reported that UBS, a global financial giant, mismanaged the trust left by her late husband by investing funds in Puerto Rican bond funds. The article reports that,

> "Tens of billions of dollars worth of bonds were issued by Puerto Rican issuers. UBS is at the forefront of the controversy. While UBS may have a defense that the funds were suitable investments at the time they were offered, the allegations in Sanchez Carmona's complaint are essentially troubling. If true, the brokerage firm intentionally lied to her and knowingly allowed a non-qualified investor – her late husband – to purchase shares in the fund.
>
> "Luckily, if the allegations are true, UBS has the financial ability to pay a $4.5 million judgment. Many small brokerage firms are grossly undercapitalized and would be wiped if just a few customers brought claims." [18]

Do not take comfort because you are dealing with a big name Wall Street investment firm. Yes, they say all the right things about how they have the best research departments, the best investment funds, the best supervision, the best results for clients, the best brokers, the best everything. And their offices and sales materials and client lists show they have been successful. But their success comes from being able to sell investments and services. It does not mean they will generate financial success for you. And it doesn't mean you are protected against losses from fraud or abuse.

A quick Google search on the firm's name along with the terms SEC or FINRA or fraud will soon lead you to information showing just how little protection you actually get from dealing with these firms.

I don't think most people would expect that a large financial services firm would intentionally lie to them but there have been many, many cases where it has happened. And as the article points out, small broker-dealers are often undercapitalized and this makes them a bigger risk. Not to be forgotten, RIA firms have also had their share of problems.

The point is that you can't close your eyes and expect any firm with access to your money and investments is going to be risk-free. Your choice of financial advisors doesn't stop at the person you are dealing with directly.

Know Who Are You Really Dealing With

With both **personal and business identity frauds** happening everywhere, are you sure you're dealing with a legitimate party? Especially if it's someone who has approached you to invest or someone you only know at a distance.

At the corporate level, have you identified the actual company that is issuing or selling you the investment? Many of the companies in the investment business have a hundred or more related companies, many with similar names. Don't assume that it doesn't matter which of these companies you are dealing with; they aren't all equally financially strong and they aren't all going to stand behind an investment. For them, it's a business and many of the related companies are set up specifically to protect the parent company from lawsuits. Just because some sales person says the parent company stands behind the products of its subsidiaries, that doesn't make it so if it's not stated in the prospectus or other written materials describing the investment.

Impersonation of a legitimate business by use of a similar sounding name has become a fairly common scam. The SEC maintains a website named Public Alert: Unregistered Soliciting Entities (PAUSE). https://www.sec.gov/investor/oiepauselist.htm

The site warns that, *"The SEC has determined that the impersonators on the list below have no connection with, and are not to be confused with, the genuine firms, whether active or defunct."* Look through these examples and notice how they resemble legitimate firms with apparently legitimate addresses.

The <u>List of Unregistered Soliciting Entities Impersonating Genuine and Former US Registered Securities Firms</u>, a*s of November 2015, included close to 200 entities. The following is a sample of the impersonators listed under the letter A.*

Alliant Holdings I Inc.
630 5th Avenue, 30th Floor
New York, NY 10111
Phone: 646-652-0720
Fax: 646-417-5423
Website:
http://www.alliantholdingsiinc.com

1. Alliant Holdings I Inc. is impersonating a genuine Regulation D exempt filer (SEC file no. 021-84296, received 060806) with the same name at the same address - Alliant Holdings I Inc. The impersonator has NO connection with, and is not to be confused with, the genuine Alliant Holdings I Inc. The SEC's EDGAR database contains filing information for the genuine entity.

American Financial Group, Inc.
1211 N. Brand Blvd., Suite 220
Glendale, CA 91202
Phone: 818-301-4918
Fax: 818-484-2163
Website:

1. American Financial Group, Inc. is impersonating a formerly registered broker-dealer with the same name - American Financial Group, Inc. (CRD Number: 10496; SEC Number: 8-26536). The genuine

http://www.amfgroupinc.com/

American Financial Group, Inc. had its registration with the Financial Industry Regulatory Authority (FINRA) cancelled, effective October 21, 1987, and is defunct.

Apex Stock Transfer Inc.
6147 S. Everett Street
Littleton, CO 80123
Phone: 720-763-9199
Fax: 720-763-9210
Website:
http://www.apexstinc.com/

1. Apex Stock Transfer Inc. is impersonating a former genuine entity having the same name (CIK Number: 0001398353; SEC Number: 084-06250). The legitimate Apex Stock Transfer Inc. filed a Form TA-W to have its registration with the SEC withdrawn, effective November 5, 2010, and is defunct. The impersonator has NO connection with, and is not to be confused with, the former genuine entity.

2. Claims to work with, or makes other reference in its solicitations to, Robbins, McCaully, Appleby LLC, a purported financial advisory services firm.

The PAUSE site contains a second list entitled, <u>List of Unregistered Soliciting Entities That Have Been the Subject of Investor Complaints</u>. https://www.sec.gov/investor/oiepauselistimpersonators.htm. This list contains close to 500 entities. The following are a small sample:

Affinity Group
Rockefeller Center Complex
45 Rockefeller Plaza
New York, NY 10111

Phone: 212-359-1692
Website: http://affinity-group.com/

Alexander Capital Management
155 N. Wacker Drive, Suite 3600
Chicago, IL 60606
Phone: 708-850-0116
Website: http://www.alexander-capital-management.com/

Alliance Group, Inc.
Alliance Insurance Agency
60 Pine Street
New York, NY 10005
Phone: 646-417-6866
Website: http://www.alliance-insagt.com/

A third list on the PAUSE website is entitled, <u>List of Fictitious Governmental Agencies and International Organizations Associated with Soliciting Entities</u>. https://www.sec.gov/investor/oiepauselistfake.htm. The following examples are from the listings under the letter B:

Board of International Equities
453 11th Street, NW
Washington, DC 20004
Website: gov.bointe.org

Board of Securities Trading Commission
1 Post Office Square, Suite 3608
Boston, MA 02109
Phone: (857) 220-8295
Website: www.bstcomm.org

Bureau of Financial Trading
1775 K Street, NW

Washington, DC (No zip)
Phone: (202) 4590965
Website: www.gov.boft.us

Bureau of International Securities Trading
912 H Street, NW
Washington, DC 20223
Phone: (202) 552-1563
Website: www.bintst.org and www.gov.bintst.org

As with all of the above examples, the names and addresses sound like they could be legitimate. It illustrates just how careful you need to be in identifying exactly who you are dealing with.

Due Diligence – Advisory Firm Risks

Your investment advisor may be self-employed but it's still likely he is part of a firm, either as an owner or employee; or is affiliated with a firm that provides various forms of support to him for a fee. The reason that this is important is because when you are performing due diligence, you need to look into the advisor's firm or affiliates as well as the advisor. Even if your advisor appears to be suitable, the firm could put your money at risk. Consider the following examples of potential exposures:

- The advisory firm's management or other employees may not be as trustworthy or suitable as the specific advisor appears to be.
- The firm may not have adequate controls to protect your funds or your private information.
- The firm may not have done adequate due diligence on the investments they recommend.
- The firm may be relying on other parties, such as a custodian, that may not be safe.

Internal Controls

Internal controls are the systems, policies and processes that an organization has in place to protect its assets and operations.

Based on its examinations of investment advisory firms the SEC has said:

> "we have learned to regard weak controls as an indicator that undetected (and uncorrected) violations may have occurred, and we have assumed that, until improved controls are implemented, investors are at risk."

Internal controls are also intended to protect your money and investments that you have passed over. For example, there should be controls to ensure one person can't authorize and issue a check on your bank account and then record it (falsely) in the accounting records. Small firms tend to have fewer controls. On the other hand, large firms often have great written procedures and other controls but they don't necessarily make sure they follow those policies. In short, you need to look at the controls and their operation in any firm that is going to have access to your money or investments to ensure your wealth isn't being put at risk.

Financial Strength

The advisor's or advisory firm's financial position, or financial strength, is also important for a couple of reasons.

First, an advisor or firm that is not reasonably strong financially is a substantial risk to you. If the firm has access to your money, which they likely will, and if they need operating funds but can't find them anywhere else, they may find the opportunity to "borrow" some of your funds too tempting to pass up.

Second, if the advisory firm is legally responsible for losses that you incur, they may not be capable of paying any legal award you might win.

On the other hand, if you are dealing with a Registered Representative of a large broker-dealer, they will have the ability to pay but that doesn't mean they will do so without a fight. Having so much money means that large broker-dealers could pay but, instead, that money is often used instead to fight your claim. **Don't assume advisory firms will accept responsibility and pay just because they are at fault.** You may think that they would want to avoid the publicity of a dispute but a review of the complaints filed against these firms will quickly show you they don't mind paying high priced lawyers to put up a good fight.

It's advisable to check the FINRA arbitration awards database for any Broker-Dealers you are considering doing business with. This can give you some insight into whether the firm settles claims fairly. This is found at http://www.finra.org/arbitration-and-mediation/arbitration-awards

....
....

Eric Dickerson – Avoidable Losses Case #4

Donald Dayton Lukens fraud scheme took somewhere around $25 million dollars from about 200 investors including numerous professional athletes. Among the victims were Eric Dickerson – Indianapolis Colts, Simeon Rice – Tampa Bay Buccaneers, D'Amarco Farr – St. Louis Rams, Shannon Sharpe - Baltimore Ravens, Sean Gilbert - Carolina Panthers, Brian Simmons - Cincinnati Bengals, Steve Atwater - Denver Broncos, Stephen Davis - Washington Redskins, Art Monk - Washington Redskins, Kurt Thomas – NBA, Byron Russell – Utah Jazz, Keith Van Horne – NBA, and Terry Norris – boxer.

According the SEC complaint,

"Central to Lukens' fraudulent schemes was the vulnerability of the customers and clients he solicited and defrauded. Lukens' victims included his pastor, fellow parishioners at his church, his children's former teacher, retirees and the disabled. These victims placed complete reliance on Lukens and entrusted him with funds they needed for retirement or for daily necessities, funds they could not afford to lose."

Lukens operated two businesses, Community Group Funding and Global Sports & Entertainment; neither of which was registered. Lukens himself was not licensed or registered to provide investment advice or to offer securities for sale.

Lukens lived life extravagantly, regularly jetting by private jet to Las Vegas, gambling heavily, driving exotic cars and hanging out with celebrities. It appeared he must have been successful in order to support his lifestyle. That and his representation that he would personally guarantee the high return investment was enough to convince investors.

According to an article about Lukens entitled *The Man Behind the Money Pit*, Lukens

"had a 17th floor office in the tallest building in Ventura County — the Financial Plaza, 300 Esplanade Drive, Oxnard — a space decorated with pictures of celebrities and athletes, including a huge screen on which he projected the images of some of his better known clients. He delighted in mentioning the celebrities with whom he had deals and associations — people like Utah Jazz forward Bryon Russell, Tampa Bay Buccaneers defensive end Simeon Rice and Monday Night Football sideline reporter Eric Dickerson. [19]

Another article about Lukens in U.S. News, *How some of the NFL's biggest stars got taken for millions*, Edward T. Pound and Douglas Pasternak, reported,

(Simeon) Rice says he emphasized that his biggest concern was preserving capital so that he would be financially secure after his playing days were finished. Lukens, he says, told him he recommended only low-risk ventures for his clients and, Rice says, "personally guaranteed each investment."

> Rice says he told Lukens he wasn't well informed about investments and "would rely on him to guide me until I learned about these matters." [20]

Rice did get a judgment for $2.4 million against Lukens but, like others, he apparently has been unable to collect.

Avoidable Losses?

Lukens was not registered to be providing investment advice or selling investments which should have been known prior to handing over any money to him. As noted above, Rice wanted to ensure his capital was preserved. In contrast, the investments Lukens was selling, including mortgage-backed securities, were very risky (and some outright scams). The problem was, as Rice said, he was relying on Lukens to do what he said. He didn't understand what was a risky investment and what was not.

As with many of the frauds against athletes and celebrities, much of the money was never invested at all. Investors' money went to Lukens or one of his companies where he had control of it. From there, it was easy to divert the money to pay his expenses. Additionally, many of the investments he sold were private and didn't have an independent custodian to hold the investments or report to the investors.

When Lukens declared bankruptcy he declared $47 million in debt; so clearly the offer of his personal guarantee was worthless. Unless a personal guarantee is backed by security with verified value and your right to that security is properly registered, a personal guarantee really means very little as far as protecting you from loss.

Could these losses have been avoided? Certainly. No one should be dealing with an unregistered investment advisor or broker and this could have been easily determined through basic due diligence on Lukens. Also, due diligence on the investments would have disclosed their high risks. Combine that with the lack of an independent custodian and the extreme lifestyle Lukens lived, and that should have removed any thought of investing with him.

What to Expect from Your Financial Advisors

If you do start your selection of your financial advisor with the due diligence described above, you will have greatly increased the chances of working with a competent and honest financial advisor. Even so, **it's a great idea to know what you should expect of your advisor, so if you aren't getting the advice and service you deserve, you will know.** Then you can get another opinion and even another advisor.

A good agent or financial advisor should provide sound financial guidance. Of course, it's hard to judge the quality of the guidance if you don't have a financial background.

What you can judge, however, is whether he is doing the things that should be done to provide sound advice. The following are characteristics or services that **you should expect from your financial advisor at the beginning of your working relationship**.

Before you agree to hire him

- Respects the confidentiality of your private information and of others as well. If you are being told about the private finances of another client, it's easy to believe that your information could be shared with others.
- Willingly acknowledges a fiduciary duty to you and is willing to put it in writing.
- Tells you if he has any potential or actual conflicts of interest before you ask.
- Asks questions about you, your family and your goals to understand your objectives.
- Explains the services he will be providing, the fees you will be paying him and any other expenses you will be billed for.
- Encourages you to ask him any questions you have, and makes sure that you understand what he is saying.

Keep in mind that financial management and investing involves a lot of industry jargon that you may not have heard before, and you shouldn't be expected to be familiar with everything. Your advisor should make you feel comfortable to ask any questions you have.

When you agree to hire him

- Reviews and explains the proposed written contract specifying the services that will be provided to you and the terms.
- The advisor may or may not suggest you have your attorney review the contract. Whether he does or doesn't suggest it, you should have the contract reviewed by an attorney. Make sure that the contract is consistent with what the advisor has said.

Initial steps upon hiring him

- Analyzes your current financial position – what you own (assets) and owe (liabilities).
- Analyzes your investments.
- Analyzes your income and expenses.
- Analyzes your tax situation.
- Explains and discusses the concept of risk tolerance with respect to investing strategy.
- Works with you to prepare a personal financial plan with objectives (discussed below).
- Works with you to develop your investment strategy and explains why it is right for you. Hopefully after reading this book you will agree that, with the uncertainty of your career length, you want a conservative strategy that will protect what you earn.
- Assists you to establish an investment account or accounts. He should explain to you the difference between cash and margin accounts. Cash accounts are standard and allow you to make investments up to the amount of money you have in the account. Margin accounts allow you to borrow against the value of the investments in your account. Margin

investing is discussed below but for now, understand that it is high risk. In addition, when you have a margin account, the brokerage firm can lend out the securities in your account which introduces a new potential risk of loss.

Ongoing

- Clearly explains the investments he recommends and how each fits into your investment strategy.
- Provides a clear statement of actual fees and expense charged each billing period.
- Provides monthly or quarterly reports of your finances.
- Explains the information in the financial reports you receive and answers clearly any questions you have.
- Maintains thorough records and supporting documents.

Financial Reporting

You should expect to be

1. Immediately informed of any changes and unexpected or unusual events so you know what is going on with your finances, and
2. Provided with understandable financial reports at least quarterly and meet personally to review them.

The financial reports/updates should start with a high-level summary of your overall financial position and schedules for your bank, investment and loan accounts similar to the following:

Suggested Personal Financial Summary

This should include a personal balance sheet showing all the things you own (assets), all the amounts (liabilities) you owe, and the amount of your equity (the amount of your assets less your liabilities. Your personal financial statement should also show a comparison to the equivalent amounts from your personal financial plan so you see whether you are progressing as you planned.

The following summaries would be a good starting point for understanding what is happening with your money.

Bank Accounts

- Bank balances, beginning of the period; $250,455.97
- Plus cash received into your bank accounts;   221,350.00
- Less cash paid out from your bank accounts; (182,988.27)
- Equals bank balances, end of the period $288,817.70

Investments

- Investments, beginning of the period; $1,595,690.22
- Plus added investment funds;   140,000.00
- Plus interest and dividends received;   17,050.00
- Less amount transferred out;   (13,269.00)
- Plus or less changes in value of investments; (32,988.27)
- Equals investments, end of the period $1,706,482.95

Loans Owed

- Loans owed, beginning of the period; $150,000.00
- Plus new loans and advances from loans;   0.00
- Plus interest and fees charged on loans   1,500.00
- Less payments on loans;   (3,500.00)
- Equals loans owed, end of the period $148,000.00

This information alone, if accurate and provided to you regularly should prevent any surprise at the end of your career. It provides a clear picture of whether you are gaining or losing wealth and can be compared to your financial plan to see if you are on track.

The financial reporting should not stop at the high-level summary above. You should also be receiving details of all transactions in each bank and investment account showing the names of each person or entity who receives a payment or pays you. If these details are grouped, you can quickly see how much you are receiving in salary, bonuses, endorsements, etc.; and how much you are spending on advisor fees, your entourage, debt payments, etc.

Finally, **you should require written reporting of any significant transactions that affect or could affect your**

finances. This will prevent later claims that you were told something that you were not. These would include, but not be limited to, details of the following:

- Terms of any loans arranged or changes in terms of existing loans;
- Any contracts entered into, amended or extended;
- Any transactions undertaken using the authority of your Power of Attorney;
- Any acquisition or disposal of assets;
- Any referral fees or other compensation received by your advisor, from 3rd parties, related to your activities or finances;
- Details of all fees charged to you by your advisor;
- Any obligations or other contingent liabilities assumed; and
- Any change in security positions arranged for your benefit.

Keep in mind that **even with good reporting from your advisor, you still should be receiving bank and loan statements directly (by mail or electronically) from your bank and investment account statements directly from the independent custodian that holds your investments.**

Watch Out for These

Manipulation Tactics

Don't fall for the tactics used by advisors or sales people who clearly just want to push you into investing in something they have to sell. When you feel that, you will likely also notice that they have made little or no attempt to really understand your situation and objectives or whether the investment would be suitable for you.

Manipulation tactics you should watch out for include:

- **Affinity** – An affinity is a feeling of closeness and trust between people because of some shared beliefs, activities, religion, purpose or other similarity. The fraudster will find something he has in common with you and use that to build trust; which is manipulated to convince you to pass over money for investments or some other purpose. This is so common that the term "Affinity Fraud" is commonly used when, for example, a member of a church uses the closeness of the congregation to create trust, for the purpose of swindling other members of the church.

- **Exclusivity** – This is a claim by a fraudster that they are the only authorized person able to offer this amazing investment, and you are one of the chosen few to be given the opportunity. They might drop names of high profile stars to suggest how lucky you are to be able to own the same investment as they do.
- **False testimonials** – This involves the use of people who are part of the fraud, or are misled, claiming they received fantastic results or providing reassurance that the investment or advice really is a great opportunity. It can also involve false claims in advertisements or brochures, or fake social media endorsements, radio shows, television and others.
- **Friendship** – The use of a request to "just trust me" should never be enough of a reason to make an investment or lend money. Anyone who says this to you clearly isn't a very smart business person and shouldn't be trusted for that reason alone. Even if their intentions were honest, their judgment puts you at risk. Perhaps they need the money because someone else just convinced them to "just trust me". The far more likely explanation is that they don't want you to look too deep into what they are supposedly trying to get you to invest in.
- **Phantom Fixation** – This scheme attempts to build up such a desirable picture of how great some investment would be if only you could get in on it. At the same time, they're telling you that it's not available. It becomes a fixation that makes you want it all the more so that you forget caution and common sense when the investment somehow does become available to you.
- **Reciprocity** – This involves manipulating you to feel an obligation to them. The most common example is the supposedly free lunch or dinner seminars often offered by

advisors trying to drum up business. These are almost always purely sales seminars where you are provided a free meal but have to listen to a presentation about some investment opportunity (ex: a timeshare). This is usually followed by pressure to buy or invest in whatever they are promoting, right then and there.   They've given you a meal; the least you can do in return is to invest in their fantastic opportunity.

- **Scarcity** – If you hear something like, "the demand has been so great that there's just room for one more a couple more people to get in on it", run away.

- **Social Consensus** - This involves claims that everyone is investing in the offered investment opportunity, so it must be good. The salesperson tells you that everyone is "getting in" – the underlying suggestion is you don't want to be the only one left out and look foolish.

- **Source Credibility** – This involves creating a belief in you that the person offering the investment obviously knows what he/she is doing; so it just makes sense to follow their advice. The credibility can be created by different means such as respected titles, professional designations, degrees from top schools, claims of their own success, company or industry awards, or by being quoted in newspapers or on television. It can also come from claims of serving high profile clients, being referred by someone you regard highly or by suggesting they are associated with some highly-regarded organization (think the big Wall Street firms).   It can also come from very professional looking brochures and websites, or very fancy offices.

One of the tricks fraudsters have used to gain credibility in a number of high profile investment frauds has been to host a radio show giving investment and other financial advice. In the case of Patrick Kiley of Minnesota, who was convicted in a $194 million investment fraud, he hosted a show called "Follow the Money" that was broadcast on the Worldwide Christian Radio network. The idea that he was also a Christian also gave people a feeling of an affinity with him in addition to the supposed credibility.

The following article excerpt is about a former leader of the National Association of Personal Financial Advisors ("NAPFA"). As you will see, his position gave him unquestioned credibility which he used to defraud his clients.

> ### Former NAPFA Chair Spangler Gets 16 Years For 'Complete Betrayal'
>
> Former NAPFA Chairman Mark Spangler has been sentenced to 16 years in prison for what the court described as "a complete betrayal" that cost his clients millions in life savings.
>
> Spangler, once a nationally prominent advisor quoted by the likes of *The Wall Street Journal* and *The New York Times*, was sentenced in U.S. District Court in Seattle on Thursday. U.S. District Court Judge Ricardo S. Martinez said at sentencing that Spangler touted his ethics and then "used his clients' trust against them," according to a press release by the Federal Bureau of Investigation.
>
> "It was a complete betrayal in the worst possible way," Martinez said. "He became willing to lie, cheat and swindle those same clients he described as friends and family."
>
> Many of his victims were long-time friends and associates, prosecutors have noted, and the money he lost represented lifelong savings earmarked for retirement, children's education and charitable giving. The prosecution indicated that in the eight months before the FBI started questioning Spangler; he spent $40,000 on boating. [21]

Here's another pretty common example of how source credibility is used. Many firms, some good and some very bad, have hired retired athletes to make introductions and establish connections, hoping the athlete's credibility transfers to them. This has been used far too often by dishonest advisors or companies to attract active players as clients, and into handing over money that is never returned. It has also landed some of those retired players in legal trouble for being involved in a fraudulent investment scheme.

- **Superior performance** – This often involves a claim by the advisor that they will get you better returns on your money, but no proof is offered and no mention is made of the risks. It works especially well for unethical advisors when their potential client is choosing between advisors they don't really know and they haven't done any due diligence on them. Human nature being what it is, most people are going to go with the advisor who claims he'll get you better results. Unfortunately, an advisor who takes this approach is more interested in getting your money than how the returns actually turn out.

> "This is the fundamental trouble facing honest people trying to make a living in the financial services industry. There is always going to be someone willing to suggest that higher returns are possible. Consumers will naturally gravitate toward whoever is offering them the best story about how they can achieve riches." [22]

Remember, **just because someone tells you, "I can do better for you" doesn't mean they will. It doesn't even mean they will try.**

- **Time pressure** – If someone trying to get you to invest in something says you have to act right now or lose the opportunity, just walk away. The pitch probably also involves an investment described as a very sweet deal for you, one they tell you that you'll be sorry if you miss out. It may also include the claim that if you decide in a day or two that it's not for you, "I'll see that you get your money back". Don't take the bait.

You should never rush into making an investment. **If you always, always make it a practice to talk over an** investment decision with someone who is not invested in or in any way involved in the investment opportunity, this will give you time to think about the opportunity sensibly and also get an objective, unbiased opinion. Hopefully you will also take the opportunity to do your due diligence on the investment before deciding whether to invest.

- **Guaranteed Returns** – These are often used to tempt investors. The target is told that there is no way to lose, or that the advisor will personally make up any shortfall in the promised returns. Legitimate registered advisors or registered representatives are prohibited legally from saying or implying an investment is guaranteed.

Advisor Red Flags

Below I have noted a number of red flags, or warning signs, of dishonest advisors or advisory firms. My experience has been that if you see these in an advisor, there's a good chance that you'll have a problem.

One of the most common red flags of advisors who are involved in frauds or embezzlement against athletes, entertainers and other high net worth individuals is their extravagant, flashy lifestyle which is often accompanied by a need for publicity. Apparently these people believe that an over the top lifestyle with all the toys of the ultra-wealthy is necessary to convince people of their (supposedly) obvious success.

Successful or not, advisors showing off an extravagant lifestyle need money from somewhere to pay for it (and it may be your accounts). **This type of behavior shows how little they value money and financial responsibility, which isn't the type of person you want looking after your money.** If they have to go over the top to show it off, it's not a good sign.

Consider the following example:

....

....

Jeffrey Rubin ran Pro Sports Financial, a financial management firm that reportedly had up to 100 athlete clients at one point. He wasn't an agent but did apparently get players referred to him by agents. Rubin provided financial services and a concierge service, handling all aspects of clients' finances, accounting, investing, bill paying etc.

Rubin had originally gained the trust of players by discovering an alleged investment Ponzi scheme run by William "Tank" Black. People assumed that because he had discovered that fraud scheme, he would be trustworthy and good at looking after their money. This was not a good assumption.

As reported in an article entitled, *Raucous lifestyle leads to fall of Jeff Rubin, former financial advisor to NFL players,* Rubin led an expensive lifestyle at the expense of his clients. He drove a Mercedes 550 and a Lamborghini (leased for $153,000). His house in Lighthouse Point in Florida cost $2.8 million but apparently was a "deal" from the developer in return for Rubin having referred some of his players, who bought houses at much higher (inflated?) prices. The same article said that according to Jason Rosenhaus, Rubin "was always with sluts who were into money. He was handing [out] money and being a flashy guy. He had the Napoleon syndrome to the 10th degree." [23] (This certainly makes you question why Rosenhaus Sports was allegedly sending some athletes to Rubin for financial management.)

According to a FINRA News Release, Rubin involved many of his clients in an investment in an illegal casino development in Alabama which was never completed, resulting in his clients losing over $40 million. Among the players who reportedly lost money in the casino development were Jevon Kearse, Terrell Owens, Plaxico Burress, Clinton Portis, Roscoe Parrish, Gerard Warren, Kyle Orton, Greg Olsen, Santonio Holmes and Santana Moss. It was also reported that Rubin received 10% of the money invested by his players in the casino as a "finder's fee".

....

....

An advisor's extravagant lifestyle is undoubtedly not a good sign. But, just because you don't see the extravagant lifestyle, it doesn't mean that you should give the advisor your unconditional trust (nor should you give it to anyone else). **The following are advisor warning signs, or red flags, that you should watch out for:**

- Over the top, free spending lifestyle that he wants everyone to see and envy;
- Braggart who constantly talks about his financial success;
- Makes unverifiable claims about making well above market profits for clients;
- Avoids answering tough questions about fees he charges;
- Has a superior attitude as though he understands financial matters that you'll never understand;
- Is a heavy gambler, drinker, or drug user or has loose morals;
- Rules don't apply to him – rules are for others;
- Tells you that you don't need to bother reading the documents he asks you to sign;
- Is okay with your free-spending and doesn't encourage financial responsibility;
- Doesn't want a written agreement stating what services he provides or terms of those services;
- Asks you to sign documents with unanswered questions or incomplete information filled in;

Here's a variation of this point. In a civil lawsuit filed against advisor Phil Kenner, NHL'er Jozef Stumpel alleged that,

"Kenner made a practice of asking Stumpel to sign documents at inopportune times and/or by presenting Stumpel with numerous documents simultaneously. Kenner pressed Stumpel - who is not a native English speaker - to sign the documents, without explaining what Stumpel was in

> fact signing and by glossing over important information about the documents."

- Only explains the positive aspects of a proposed investment, not the risks;
- Guarantees you that you won't lose on the investment;
- Tells you that you have to keep the investment opportunity confidential and can't discuss it with anyone;
- Insists on being your only point of contact at his firm;
- Discourages investments in publicly traded stocks and bonds;
- Advises you to sell the investments you currently own and invest in other products, without having prepared a financial plan for you or analyzed the tax consequences of selling what you own;
- Can't explain how the investment makes money so that you understand;
- Doesn't provide printed materials describing the investment or says there are none;
- Offers to sell you a private investment from a private source, not through the firm he/she works for (referred to as *selling away*).
- Uses a personal email instead of his business email for certain investments;
- When investing, requests you make your check payable to him personally;
- Shows preferential treatment to some clients, not treating them all the same;
- Doesn't use an independent custodian to hold your investments;
- Encourages investing on margin;

- Requests that you give him an unlimited Power of Attorney, rather than one limited to the specific thing that needs to be done and to a limited time period;

- Offers to be trustee of trusts set up to hold your assets, or to be an Officer of companies you invest in;

- Requests a loan from you or other clients;

- Has your bank and investment statements sent to his address rather than yours.

- Tries to get you to cash in an existing annuity to roll over into a new annuity.

On the other hand, don't be fooled by outward appearances. What you see or hear may be done purely to convince you to invest. Consider the following:

- Charitable giving provides good publicity. Almost all the big Ponzi schemes have been run by someone who has been a big donator to charitable causes. Bernie Madoff and Tom Petters are two who really used charitable donations to build a positive profile in their communities.

- Payment of the first interest or profits due to investors builds trust. It's common for investors in Ponzi schemes to receive the expected first payment. Investors see this as proof the investment is legitimate and will often invest more when asked and vouch for its legitimacy to new potential investors.

- Many advisors publicly display the appearance of devout Christianity. Unfortunately, this is often just a façade to gain your trust and is definitely not reason to forego proper independent diligence (i.e. background research) on him.

Summary

Many clients believe their agent, business manager or financial advisor is knowledgeable about exposures to their financial security and are taking steps to protect their interests, particularly from fraud and embezzlement. In reality, most of these agents, business managers or financial advisors do very little (if anything) to assess and take steps to mitigate the risks of fraud and embezzlement.

Remember the three principals mentioned above:

1. Your advisors should put in writing that they will have a fiduciary duty to put your interests first. You still must investigate the advisor's competence, regulatory record and character.
2. Have the contract(s) with your advisor(s) state exactly what services your advisor is responsible for providing and don't assume they are doing anything more. If they are responsible for protecting your financial interests, get the specifics in writing.
3. Do not let one person or firm have control over all of your financial affairs. Any person or firm having access to your bank accounts, investments or other assets should not be doing your accounting or taxes.
4. Do not let any person or firm handle any part of your financial affairs without oversight i.e. you or someone independent monitoring what they are doing.

Part IV – Investing

A Brief Explanation of Investing

Investing is essentially comprised of two types of transactions. They are:

1. Purchasing something with the expectation that will earn money for you and/or its value will increase over time, and
2. Lending money to a government,company, or person with the expectation of being paid interest for the use of the money until it is returned.

There are countless variations of investment products within these two basic types of investments and some that combine characteristics of both.

Some investments are much safer than others, but always keep in mind that when investing, there are no sure things.

Are You Investing, Trading or Betting?

Just because you put your money into some investment products doesn't mean you are investing. And neither does having an investment account at a brokerage house, buying stocks online, or buying gold. Having a financial advisor making the decisions for you doesn't necessarily mean you are investing either. **Whether you are investing, trading or betting depends on what you buy or sell, why you bought or sold it, and what you intend to do with it**.

For those of us concerned about our financial security, it does make a big difference whether we are investing as opposed to trading or betting (speculating). If you are investing following accepted strategies the chances are very good that over a longer term you will grow your investments. If you are trading or betting, you may have some good results from time to time, but over a longer period there is a good chance you won't even break even.

This is not to say that if it's in your nature to take greater risks than most that you should never trade or take a chance by purchasing shares in a company you think will be a big success. **If you need to take a flier, just don't make your bet with money you are counting on for your retirement or money you can't afford to lose.**

Trading

Many people believe that investing means trading stocks and that you can make more money by trading more. Why wouldn't you believe that? Have you watched Jim Cramer on TV? Callers ask questions about specific stock picks and hear "Buy, buy, buy" or "Sell, sell, sell". Watch CNBC and they tell you what stocks are hot right now. Analysts working for investment banks research individual stocks then issue recommendation about whether you should buy, sell or hold them.

If you go to Scottrade's website, you quickly see that you should have an account with them because, "Stock trading is affordable with $7 online trades for most stocks, easy-to-use tools at no extra charge and the ability to trade unlimited shares."

At TD Ameritrade's website home page, you see that they offer "Free, powerful trading programs" and "Trade commission free for 60 days. Get up to $600."

Here are a few other examples of how the industry tries to influence you to trade more.

- "We'll provide insight into what companies to buy and which to sell"
- "Our platform can help you make decisions"
- "The latest techniques for determining which way the market will go"
- "How to use options to increase your profit"

All of these messages suggest that everyone is trading and that must be what investing is.

But keep in mind that brokers have mega dollars to spend to publicize the idea that you should be trading, and they make a lot of money off people who trade. What is good for them is not good for you.

If you are trading, research shows that you will not do well over time. Even full-time professionals who have access to sophisticated research and tools do not succeed consistently. If you are regularly trading securities, commodities or currencies, trying to make profits by buying and selling, and think that's the way to accumulate wealth, you are misinformed.

Betting, Speculating or Gambling

Who hasn't seen articles about startup companies making millions for early investors? We'd all like to be one of those investors. But don't forget that, other than the people who built those companies, the other investors were generally venture capitalists investing with other peoples' money. They are in the business of investing in early stage companies, and they get to see the inside workings of the startup before investing. It's also true that they lose their entire investment in a company far more often than they make the huge profits on a company like we all dream of doing.

Who doesn't have a story about some company they thought of investing in on the spur of the moment, but didn't, and whose stock then skyrocketed; leaving them feeling like a loser again. Keep in mind that there are many, many more people who have made that spur of the moment investment only to see the stock plummet. Spur of the moment decisions to invest, or decisions made solely on the basis of urging by anyone, very seldom work out well.

A recent advertisement offered, "The latest techniques for determining which way the market will go…" If you follow any strategy that depends on predicting the markets direction in the short term, you are betting. No one knows what the markets will do in the short term. The risks are huge. Your odds are likely better in Las Vegas.

You Can't Predict Investment Performance

What is the stock market going to do tomorrow, next week, a month from now;? What about the real estate market?

Are the shares of a particular company going up or down tomorrow, next week, a month from now, any time?

Which stocks are going to be the best performers in the coming year?

What is going to happen to interest rates and how will the bond market react?

You don't know the answers but neither does anyone else, no matter what they say. Some people may have more data and knowledge of past performance, company operations and management, but even with that advantage, data shows that no one can consistently predict future performance. Even Warren Buffett says,

> "We've long felt that the only value of stock forecasters is to make fortune tellers look good. Even now, Charlie [Munger] and I continue to believe that short-term market forecasts are poison and should be kept locked up in a safe place, away from children and also from grown-ups who behave in the market like children."

If it's not possible to predict with certainty what's going to happen with particular investments, the logical strategy is to spread your money across multiple investments, but not just any investments. Avoid high risk investments where you can suffer large permanent losses.

Asset Allocation and Asset Classes

Minimizing your risks of permanent significant loss begins with determining how you want to allocate your investable dollars between the asset classes. This is commonly referred to as asset allocation. An asset allocation is a statement of how much of your money you want in each class of investments. As an example, an allocation might include:

- 60% in publicly traded stocks,
- 30% in fixed income securities, and
- 10% in cash.

Descriptions of the asset classes are found in Appendix 5.

Your allocation should be based on your risk tolerance, your age, how much you already have saved for retirement, what your financial target is, etc. This is why, if your advisor doesn't sit with you to understand you and what's important to you, you don't have the best advisor.

Your asset allocation should be developed as part of your personal financial plan, in conjunction with your financial advisor. It should consider your particular circumstances such as age, years to retirement, comfort with risk and anticipated career earning pattern.

Why not just stick with the best performing asset class? First, you can't predict which will be the best performing asset class from year to year. Second, your risk is higher with just one class. Third it will have you chasing the asset class with the best returns in the past year or two (remember that past performance is not an indicator of future performance). None of this will work in your favor.

If preservation of your wealth is a priority and you have multiple years to hold your investments, the majority of your money should be invested in publicly traded stocks and fixed income securities. When you have grown your investments to more than you need to live the life you want in retirement, then you can consider some of the riskier asset classes. Just be aware that there is a much greater risk that you will permanently lose your investment in many of those other asset classes.

Once you have settled on an asset allocation, the next step is ensuring you have diversification within each asset class.

Diversification

Diversification is the opposite of concentration in your investments, which appears to have been a factor in Antoine Walker's bankruptcy discussed above. It involves spreading your investable money into multiple investments in the asset classes you have selected in your asset allocation. Diversification is the key to investing while minimizing your risk of suffering a significant loss of wealth.

Diversification itself doesn't reduce the risk of failure of any particular investment, but it does reduce the financial impact on your financial security if one does fail. If you have invested in 5 or 10 or 30 different investments the maximum loss on any one investment will be lower as the number of investments grows larger.

Diversification within an asset class can be achieved in a couple of ways. For example, in publicly traded stocks, you can purchase a broad range of good quality individual stocks, but this takes time to research which are the best quality stocks and to monitor them after you have purchased them. Another choice is to buy **mutual funds or exchange traded funds** ("ETF's"). With either of these, you invest in the fund where a manager selects which companies to buy (within certain guidelines) and how much to invest in each. So you might say in your asset allocation that you want 10% invested in a large cap fund, one that only invests in the largest companies. The large cap fund manager purchases shares of most or perhaps all of the large cap companies. Since you have a piece of the mutual fund, you effectively have a piece of every one of those large cap companies. There are thousands of mutual funds and ETF's to choose from but their main benefit is the ability to obtain diversification at a low cost.

When purchasing mutual funds or ETF's, be aware that diversification is not achieved by buying two or more mutual funds or ETF's in the same asset class but from different companies or fund managers. For instance, if you invest $10,000 in a large cap mutual fund from, say, Vanguard and another $10,000 in a large cap mutual fund from i-Shares, you are not more diversified than if you put the total of $20,000 in either one.   There may be differences in the operating expenses of each, but the stocks held in each fund will be essentially the same.

Passive vs Active Management

Passive investing involves selecting your asset allocation, choosing your diversified investments within those classes and, other than rebalancing discussed in the next section, sticking with what you have. Active management involves the investment fund manager buying and selling certain investments as conditions change or as he/she believes there is an opportunity for better returns. While this sounds like a good idea, overall results over many years have shown that active management does not provide better results. And active management has higher operating costs which reduce the returns you receive.

Rebalancing

Rebalancing is a concept that is applied to your asset allocation. Think of rebalancing this way: you are trying to maximize your investment results by periodically selling some of the assets classes that have gone up in value (sell high) and using that money to purchase more of the asset classes that have either gone down or not increased as much (buy low).   Let's say you started with an asset allocation of 70% of your money in publicly traded stocks and 30% in fixed income securities; but over the next year stocks went up and bonds went down. You ended the year with 75% of your investment dollars in stocks and 25% in bonds.   In order to get back to the 70%-30% asset allocation you started with, you would sell stocks and buy fixed income securities.

Rebalancing is very important to growing your investment portfolio. History has shown that returns from different asset classes vary over time. By figuring out at the beginning what is the best asset allocation for you, rebalancing at least annually to maintain that same asset allocation has historically provided better returns than not rebalancing.

Other Promoted Investing Strategies

There are other investing strategies that are promoted as ways to achieve higher returns. These are riskier than deciding on an asset allocation and being diversified within those classes. If your advisor is intent on following these, the odds are very good that you are paying higher fees and earning lower returns than by following a solid asset allocation strategy using low cost funds. I put these here so that you know to avoid them.

- Stock Picking – This involves researching and selecting companies that the picker believes will outperform the other companies in the market. They consider the general economic conditions, each company's particular strengths and weaknesses, and buy just the shares of the companies they believe will do better. Again, the evidence shows that this works for some stock pickers but not for most; and not consistently for any.

- Short Selling – This occurs when someone believes a company or sector's share prices are going to fall. They will borrow shares of that company or sector and sell them at today's price. If, and when, the share price does fall, the short seller will buy shares and return them to the broker–dealer they borrowed them from. In this way, they hope to sell at a high price then later replace them at a lower price, profiting from the difference in price less the costs of borrowing the shares.

- Timing the Market – This refers to buying shares of specific companies before their price goes up, and selling before the price falls. No-one can predict the market successfully and this strategy doesn't beat the market consistently.

- Chasing Hot Sectors or Hot Asset Managers – This involves identifying sectors of the economy that are doing well and are expected to continue to do so. The problem is that anyone can see what sector or market has been hot. No-one can consistently tell which ones will stay hot. Many people will jump into a sector that has been hot only to find that the hot streak has finished and they have bought at the peak prices. Hot managers can become celebrities in the financial world and people will jump to invest in their funds. However, one of the most referenced truths of investing, but also one of the least accepted, is that **Past Performance is Not an Indicator of Future Performance**. Believe it!

- Momentum investing – This is somewhat like timing the market. It involves an assumption that shares that are moving consistently upward in price (with momentum) will continue to do so. Different investors or investment fund managers will have different criteria for what qualifies as momentum and when the momentum has stopped and it's time to sell. As with the other strategies, this is not a consistent winning strategy.

Annuities

Annuities are contracts with insurance companies whereby you give them money and they guarantee to pay you an income for a specified period of time. Annuities are generally known for charging high fees but some types may be worth considering if you want to put money out of reach for a longer period.

Fixed deferred annuities offer a minimum fixed interest rate with tax free growth for a specified period. The idea is that you can put the money away while you are earning it and then receive payments when you retire. These contracts are very complicated and are not written to favor you over the issuer. If you do decide on one of these, it is very important to clearly understand the terms and fees, and what will happen with the money if you die.

Variable or indexed annuities are essentially a way to invest in the stock market inside an insurance contract so that gains, if any, are tax free. However, the fees are very high and while they may protect you from losing principal in a down market, you are likely restricted in how much you benefit no matter how well your investments do. These are generally not recommended by advisors who have a fiduciary duty to put your interests above theirs.

In addition to high ongoing fees, all types of annuities likely will have a lock-in period during which you can't withdraw money from the annuity without paying a high fee. These fees may last ten or more years.

Remember as well, the company issuing the annuities has to still be around and in business when you want to receive money in the future. This means that they have to be very strong financially and be monitored for any changes in its credit rating, ownership or other negative factors. If the company does become insolvent or bankrupt, you may not get the payments you were expecting.

As noted above, one problem with annuities is the high fees charged. Another is the high commissions paid to the person who sells it to you. Many clients have been convinced to cash out one annuity to invest in a supposedly superior annuity. This is generally very costly to the client and is a red flag you should not ignore.

Considerations When Selecting Investments

The following paragraphs are not about to tell what investments to make but are important considerations when you are selecting investments.

Registered Investments

Investments that are publicly traded on exchanges must be **registered** with and are regulated by the SEC or state regulators. Companies wanting to register securities (investments) must provide detailed historic audited information about the company and the investment opportunity. In addition, the company must provide investors with a Prospectus, which includes audited financial statements of the company, discussions by management of the risks involved, information on ownership and much more. Regulators review this information and determine whether the investment can be registered.

Exempt Investments

Certain investments that are intended only to be sold to Accredited Investors or to a limited number of investors can be given **exempt** status by the SEC.   Much more limited information must be provided to the regulators about the investment opportunity, but if it meets required criteria, it will be exempt from full registration. Unfortunately exempt investments are often used in fraudulent schemes.

Unregistered Investments

Unregistered investments are neither registered nor exempted by the SEC or state regulators. If the investment offered to you is unregistered, your risk of permanent loss is way too high. Realize that you are taking a real gamble and are very likely to lose your investment.

Fees and Expenses

A Path to Retirement, for Those Far From It

Like John C. Bogle, the founder of Vanguard, whom he admires, Mr. Bernstein views Wall Street as a largely parasitic enterprise that flourishes at the expense of ordinary investors. "You are engaged in a life and death struggle with the financial services industry," he warns in the pamphlet.

"Every dollar in fees and expenses you pay them comes directly out of your pocket." [24]

The biggest differentiator of how well you will do in two investment funds with similar holdings is the amount of fees and expenses each fund charges. The fees and expenses include the sales charges (what you are charged to invest in the fund or to leave the fund), if any, and operating expenses of the fund. You should not even consider those funds that charge you sales charges or "loads" of any kind.   Then when deciding between similar funds that have no sales charge ("no-load funds"), the one with the lower operating expenses will usually do better for you.

Investment Due Diligence: Research and Evaluation

The biggest investors include pension funds, private equity funds, corporations, foundations, etc.   One thing they have in common is that they undertake due diligence on any investment before actually passing over their money. Many of these organizations don't have employees to perform the due diligence so they use external legal and consulting firms.

The purpose of due diligence is to ensure that the risks and potential return of the investment opportunity are identified and thoroughly assessed. The due diligence will depend on what the specific investment is, but generally due diligence will evaluate at least:

- Management
- Finances
- Strategy
- Transparency
- Operations
- Competitive position
- Total fees to purchase, maintain, and sell the investment

There are many other areas. Due diligence is not a casual exercise; it is a thorough investigation. Someone's word or a "trust me" isn't going to cut it. Good investors know that risks exist that may not have been disclosed to them and that the opportunity may not be quite as good as represented.

If large organizations undertake thorough due diligence when making an investment that may be only a small fraction of their total investments, it makes sense that an individual who is investing his/her hard-earned funds would want to be just as certain about their investments.

Most individuals who work in areas other than finance won't know which due diligence procedures to undertake or, in many cases, whether the information they collect is reliable or the implications of that information.

Appendix 7 is an example due diligence questionnaire to assist you in collecting information about investment opportunities that you are considering.

Keep in mind that any questionnaire, checklist or work program can only go so far in anticipating or identifying issues and risks. Also, the questionnaire is only a tool for gathering information. This is not necessarily comprehensive of everything you might want to evaluate because that will depend on factors specific to you and to the investment. It is meant as an aid to illustrate the type of information you should be assessing. The analysis of the information and assessment of the investment opportunity is where knowledge and experience really make a difference.

I suggest that you use the checklist as an aide as follows:

1. Gather the information and do your own initial assessment;
2. If your assessment is that the investment opportunity doesn't feel right, turn it down; but
3. **If it does seem to be a good opportunity, consult with a professional for a second opinion before committing to the investment.**

Warren Buffett wrote in his 2014 shareholders letter:

> "You don't need to be an expert in order to achieve satisfactory investment returns. But if you aren't, you must recognize your limitations and follow a course certain to work reasonably well. Keep things simple and don't swing for the fences."

If your goal is preservation of your investments, there are two warnings you should not violate. If you can't understand how the investment makes or loses money, don't invest. And if the investment isn't transparent so that you can follow and verify where your money goes and how it is used (i.e. it seems your money disappears into a black box and you find out at the end if you won or lost), don't invest. If you aren't clear on these concepts consider the following two examples, reflecting these two warnings.

First, there is an exchange-traded product (ETP) that tracks the inverse of the performance of futures on the CBOE Volatility Index or VIX. You'd have to be a genius to understand that one.

Second example is an Absolute Return Fund. Absolute return funds basically have no restrictions on what they can invest in. The idea is that they try to achieve a certain return, say 7%, by trying to find some way to invest and make that return. The problem is that it's not like you are guaranteed a 7% return; "absolute" only means they are going to try to make 7%. And they don't tell you how. It's that black box and definitely not a conservative investment.

Conflicting Information

There is more than enough information about investing available to anyone who has a computer and the desire to learn (and a lot of time), but you may have noticed that for every opinion or piece of advice you find someone else is expressing the exact opposite opinion. What should you believe when both sound convincing?

Even worse, the investment advice or opinions you come across in media are often deliberately slanted to try to convince you a product or strategy is in your best interest when it is not! What you can be sure of is that just because you see it on a website, or in an article, or hear it on the radio or television doesn't mean you should accept it as true.

Summary

If you are investing following accepted strategies and investing in publicly traded securities, the chances are very good that over a longer term you will grow your investments. If you are trading or speculating/betting, you may have some good results from time to time, but over a longer period there is a good chance you won't even break even.

You can reduce your chances of large permanent losses if you have an asset allocation that suits your present situation and objectives, are diversified within asset classes, and rebalance your investments at least annually.

The amount of fees and expenses you pay will make a big difference in the investment growth you will achieve over time. The additional fees you would be charged for active investment management generally result in lower returns for you.   Make sure you know all the fees you will be paying when considering investments, and when selecting between similar investment funds go for the one with the lower fees and expenses.

Part V – High Risk and Fraudulent Investments

All investments have risk. If the investment is legitimate, you can be confident that the higher the potential return, the higher the risk of a major loss of your money. Certain investments are incredibly high risk, whether legitimate or not, and you should be very skeptical of these no matter how good they seem to be.

Investments for Accredited or Sophisticated Investors

As a professional athlete or entertainer you may meet the criteria to be considered an Accredited Investor. In order to meet the criteria you need a net worth of $1 million excluding your primary residence and an income of greater than $200,000 or $300,000 as a couple for the two prior years and likely to make at least this much in the current year. But meeting those criteria doesn't magically mean you know anything more about investing than before you got the big contract and suddenly were considered to meet those criteria. **The danger of being an Accredited Investor is that advisors or other investment sales people can legally try to sell you certain higher risk investments that don't need to be registered with the SEC.** If you weren't accredited they wouldn't be allowed, by regulation, to be trying to sell these products to you. The products are generally very good for the sales people because they receive large commissions for selling them to you. But the products are much less likely to be good for your finances. At worst, you will lose all your investment. At best, any returns you receive will be after large fees have been paid. And remember, these may say they'll provide big returns, but this means big risk.

Binary Options (Fraudulent)

Binary Options are generally sold by telephone from foreign countries or websites. They are not just high risk; they are fraudulent.

Commodities and Commodities Trading Accounts

Commodities are materials such as wheat, oil and gas, coal, lumber, metals and other physical goods that are bought and sold, often in large quantities. Major buyers are companies that need these for their businesses and have departments of professionals who monitor supply and demand around the globe and around the clock to get the best prices and quality.

There are also traders who buy and sell options contracts, or "futures", which specify how much of a commodity is to be delivered at a specified price at a specified future date. These are called futures contracts and can be traded without ever having to take possession of the actual commodity.

I doubt your advisor would legitimately recommend that you trade these options. However, you might be approached to invest your money in Commodities Trading Accounts. You'll be told a very experienced trader can make amazing returns with little risk due to his knowledge of the markets. Once again, the opportunity for high returns means high risk so he's misleading you even if he does invest your money. Unfortunately many of these opportunities to have someone else trade options with your money are scams and you will lose all of your investment.

How investors lose 89% of gains from futures funds

October 8, 2013 - 9:05 am EST

According to data filed with the Securities and Exchange Commission and compiled by Bloomberg, 89% of the $11.51 billion in gains in 63 managed-futures funds went to fees, commissions and expenses during the decade from Jan. 1, 2003, to Dec. 31, 2012.

Brokers have an incentive to keep clients in managed-futures funds because they receive commissions annually of up to 4% of assets invested, prospectuses show. Investors pay as much as 9% in total fees each year, including charges by general partners and fund managers.

> **The Grant Park Futures Fund reported a net investor loss of $68.6 million during the 10-year period through Dec. 31, after paying fees and commissions of $427.7 million.** [30]

FOREX ("Foreign Exchange" or "Currency Trading")

Different countries have different currencies and those currencies change in value against the U.S. dollar. By buying and selling different currencies you can make money if you can guess which ones are going up and which down, but that is a risky bet. Further, it seems that a large number of FOREX investments offered to individuals are scams. Consider this:

In September 2013 a press release was issued by a forex trader. It was entitled, *Forex: The Bank of the Future - Secureinvestment.com.* In part, it read,

> SecureInvestment.com is one of the top investment companies providing managed Forex accounts to investors. The company specializes in such service that *assures clients of their profits*. What makes their services even better is that investors can easily *open an account online through the company's website*. After that, *they can immediately fund their account* depending on the investment package that they choose. Secure Investment's packages are also varied so clients can choose a package that matches their budget.
>
> Managed Forex account is *just like putting one's money in the bank*. Instead of getting the trifling interest with your money, one can *get double or even triple the amount of initial investment*. This definitely is the right way to earn and save money. *Aside from the fast and big returns*, Secure Investment *also assures all their clients that the losses are covered*. They made investing a not so risky game. (Italics were added for emphasis.) [34]

The above press release and other promotion obviously did a very good job. The next year, on Bloomberg's website, the headline read, *Forex Investors May Face $1 Billion Loss as Trade Site Vanishes.*

> Customers in 11 countries on five continents say they have seen their money evaporate with Secure. Twenty-five investors interviewed say Secure, which was incorporated in Panama in 2008, had instructed them to wire money to banks in Australia, Cyprus, Latvia and Poland. [35]

Secureinvestment was clearly a well thought out sophisticated crime. They didn't have a physical office and it still isn't known where the website was actually located. Investors were told to wire funds to banks in a dozen countries, but those accounts would operate only a short time before being closed. Clients who requested small withdrawals to test the legitimacy of the site received checks, but larger withdrawal requests were stalled continually. They (whoever they were) even offered people the opportunity to start investing without money. By referring someone to them who subsequently invested at least $500, they would pay you $200 you could use to invest (and lose).

Besides suffering a loss, one investor realized that might not be the end of his troubles. He posted, "Do not forget that the criminals behind secureinvestments.com stole our money but also have all the identification papers we sent over to open our accounts. Passports, bank accounts etc...are in the hands of a criminal organization."

The scammers have not been caught and no money has been recovered.

High Yield Investment Products ("HYIP's")

These include products that are totally fraudulent, using high returns to lure in investors; and also include legitimate investments that have to pay high interest rates because they are so risky. The first category of course are fraudulent; the second are probably unsuitable for most people, or are only suitable as a small part of your investment portfolio.

Liquid Alternatives

Alternative investments have been around for years but generally they have only been offered to foundations or pensions because of the high minimum amount that had to be invested. Alternative investments include many different types of investments using different strategies. They gained popularity after some of these investments hit homeruns and produced huge returns that were all over the news, but the reality is that most alternatives do not perform as well as the overall stock market. However, because of the interest created by the big wins, the industry developed liquid alternatives which allow smaller investors to pool their money with a manager who then invests in alternative investments.

Among others, one of the problems is that there has been a halo effect created by some of the publicized big wins by alternative investment funds. Now investors hear the word alternatives and immediately associate it with their opportunity to get in on the big returns they have read about. The track record doesn't justify the risk. But if you do decide to take a chance, remember that all alternative investments, and liquid alternatives, are not equal. Extensive due diligence should be undertaken before speculating with your money on one of these. You'll find there are many more losers than winners.

Master Limited Partnerships

Master Limited Partnerships ("MLP's") are generally sold as investments that offer large pay outs annually and offer some tax advantages to certain investors. The payouts are often financed by the MLP borrowing money, which lowers the value of your investment. So instead of getting dividends or interest from a company's profits, the MLP may be paying you out of loans. Also, many if not most of these investments are associated with oil and gas related companies that have seen their prices fall along with the price of oil. Recently, a number of these MLP's have declared bankruptcy when their cash flow fell to a point where they could not pay their obligations.

Mortgage Backed Securities

These are the investments that are often blamed for creating the financial crisis in 2008. Supposedly the securities are secured or "backed" by mortgages (or other forms of debt) that pay interest. However, it is pretty well impossible for you as an investor to know the quality of the mortgages or other debt you are relying on for the interest and safety of your investment. Because of their lack of transparency and complexity they are very high risk.

Non-Traded REITs

Real Estate Investment Trusts are set up to pool investors' money to invest in real estate of all types. Some of these REITs are publicly traded and can be bought or sold like other publicly traded investments. There are also closed-end funds or non-traded REITs that require you to invest money for extended periods. If you can sell them at all, it is likely only if you can find another investor to sell to in a private transaction. These generally are very risky, tie up your money for long periods and have high fees.

Oil & Gas

There are numerous ways to invest in oil and gas; some are legitimate and some are fraudulent. Unless you are investing in publicly traded large cap oil companies such Exxon or British Petroleum, be very cautious of being defrauded. Even if you do some due diligence, part of the problem is being able to evaluate the legitimacy of the investment opportunity; the other is being able to evaluate the people involved. If you are interested in preserving your wealth through conservative investing, oil and gas isn't your answer.

Penny and Micro-cap Stocks

Penny and micro-cap stocks are basically stocks that sell for around a dollar or two a share and are usually traded **Over the**

Counter, or OTC. These are speculative and very risky at best and often are the stocks that are pumped up by salespeople operating out of boiler rooms in classic pump and dump schemes.

Peer to Peer Lending

Peer to peer lending is an internet facilitated way for people who need to borrow money and people who have money to lend to negotiate direct loans, without any banks involved. Recently one of the largest peer to peer lending businesses in China was found to be a huge Ponzi fraud. It was reported that the company had operated for a few years and had defrauded lenders of over $6 billion. Apparently, very few if any of the borrowers were real. Since there was never any direct meetings between the borrowers and lenders, and lenders relied on what was shown to them over the internet, it was easy to create imaginary businesses to borrow money.

Prime Bank Notes

If you are being offered the opportunity to invest in prime bank notes, it is a scam, no question. These offer high returns in a short period by supposedly reselling notes guaranteed by "prime" banks. These are often sold as being exclusive and used by European royal families and therefore require confidentiality. Of course, it's all lies. You're told to either give your money to the promoter directly, or to an offshore location, i.e. outside the U.S. Then your money is never seen by you again.

Promissory Notes

As mentioned earlier, promissory notes are basically written promises to pay you back for money you have loaned to a person or company, with interest. They are unsecured loans so if you are not repaid, you can sue the person who gave you the note, but you will likely just be another person in a long line of creditors hoping to be paid. Promissory notes can be offered privately between individuals, but if they are offered as investments, they generally should be registered with the SEC; and always avoided if you want to preserve your wealth.

Private Placements

Private Placements are offerings of a company's securities that are exempt from registration with the SEC under Regulation D, Rule 506 and are not offered to the public at large. They have limited regulatory oversight and are intended for accredited investors.

Private placements are very high risk, even when legitimate. They have been the instrument of many investment frauds and are certainly not considered conservative investments.

As stated in the NASAA Enforcement 2014 Report on 2013 Data,

> "Unregistered securities sold by unlicensed individuals continue to attract the most attention from state regulators. These fraudulent offerings are increasingly being marketed through the Internet."

Structured Products

Structured products are pre-packaged investments whose performance depends on the performance of some other investment product or group. As a group, these are complicated investments that have resulted in many major losses and lawsuits.

Virtual or Digital Currencies

Virtual or digital currencies such as Bitcoin are a recent development and some people have used the idea of getting in on the ground floor as a pitch to get you to buy.

These digital currencies are very new and are not well understood. Although in theory digital currencies may have some advantages over traditional currencies, investing in them now is very speculative. Not only are they not transparent (i.e. you can't see or verify how they work), they have had some significant problems with thefts and frauds already. It is likely that if you were allowed to perform due diligence, you would find these too risky for comfort.

Summary

The above investments are all high risk, however some are legitimate and have some chance of earning a return on your investment, and some are simply ways to steal your money.   If you do enough research to know they are legitimate and you want to take a chance, just be sure not to use money you need and is not more than one or two percent of your investments.

Part VI – Planning and Implementation

You may ask, why do I need a financial plan? Here are a few reasons:

- You won't work forever. In fact, your prime earning years may be far fewer than your retirement years. At some point (hopefully after your career is over) you are going to be spending more than you are earning, and you need to have an idea of how much you will have to save to meet your needs.
- You probably have other goals besides just being able to have enough for retirement. You may want to help your kids pay for college, look after your parents or maybe start a foundation to support a charitable enterprise and leave a legacy.
- Making a plan gives you a benchmark so periodically you can compare how you are actually doing against it. When you compare where you are to where you should be you may find you are behind. It's your choice at that point whether you want to change what you are doing with your money, but at least you will be alerted if you are falling behind and will be able to tell if it's because of poor investment returns, saving too little or spending too much.
- A financial plan should save you taxes. You can't just wait until the end of each year and then expect to be able to magically reduce what you owe to the government, but through financial planning you can minimize the amount you owe in taxes.

A personal financial plan is your financial playbook. Your financial advisor should have gone through the process of gathering information from you and working with you to prepare your personal financial plan, and should update it at least annually.

- Key information in your personal financial plan should include
    - Your current net worth (the value of what you own minus what you owe);

- Your financial and other goals, which will generally include the amount you will need to retire plus things such as paying for college tuition for your children, future health care costs and other potential needs. The process should also consider what you are planning to do after you retire and any costs associated with preparing for that second career;
- The difference between what you have now and what you want to have at the end of your career is the amount you need to accumulate, which should be planned out by year.
- Your financial plan should break out how you can meet each year's target increase in your net worth from
  - Savings from your earnings; and
  - Investment returns.
- Then, at a minimum, each year you and your advisor should compare your personal financial plan to what has actually happened, and then your plan should be updated to reflect changes that have taken place.

It is very important to understand that **the most important factor in determining how well off you and your family will be after you retire is how much you save each year** (assuming you avoid losing your savings and investments). If you don't save while you are earning, there is no investment that will make up for that at the end.

Your Investment Strategy

Once you have the information on how much you will need to accumulate from your plan, you will also need an investment strategy specifying what types of investments you will use to earn the returns you need (this doesn't mean that you can simply say you want to earn a return of say, 20%, and there will be a strategy to earn that amount. Even the highest available returns on legitimate investments will reflect the rates in the market for similar high-risk investments. If the rate offered is higher than the market rate, it probably means the investment is not legitimate.)

Your investment strategy should consider the following:

- What is the purpose of your investment?

As athletes, you have an uncertain (and often short) career to try to accumulate enough wealth to be able to support you, or supplement other income you may earn, after your sports career and into retirement.

- What are your investment goals?

Your investment goals may vary depending on such things as your age, how much you need to accumulate, what the investment is for, whether you're supporting a family, etc.

Not all of your investment funds are necessarily used to meet the same goals. For instance:

- You may already have accumulated the amount you need for retirement and so you primarily want to preserve these funds in low risk investments.
- You may have other funds you want to invest in something that will produce income in the form of interest or dividends.
- You may have other funds you want to use to leave a legacy gift to some institution or charity when you pass, and you may be willing to take a higher risk with these funds in the hope of leaving a much larger legacy.
- What is your time horizon? This refers to the periods of time you need to consider in your investment plan. For example,
  - During your playing career, you should be accumulating wealth and adding to your investments. Even though you may not need these funds in the near future, you want to ensure they invested conservatively, not going for the home run by locking your funds into some high-risk long-term venture.
  - After you have finished playing, if you have no other source of income, you will need to generate cash in order to pay your living expenses. The cash may

come from interest or dividends from your investments, from selling investments or from selling other things you own.

- o Some investments such as publicly traded company shares are very liquid, meaning you can easily sell them to get cash out whenever you need it. Other investments are illiquid, meaning you may be locked into holding them for months or years, or in some cases there just isn't anyone interested in buying your investment except perhaps at a fire sale price.

- What is your tolerance to risk?
  - o When an advisor asks you about your risk tolerance, they are generally referring to how you feel when investments decrease in value. Are you comfortable waiting for them to recover or do you panic and want to sell as soon as there is any kind of decrease?
  - o What sometimes gets missed in this assessment is a discussion of your comfort with temporary losses versus permanent losses. Unfortunately, there are investments that have a much higher chance of permanent losses than others. You shouldn't have much tolerance for these types of investments.
  - o If you are investing in something that goes up and down in price but over the long term grows its underlying value (for example, the stock market), you should have a higher tolerance to this risk.
  - o If preservation of your financial security is your goal, you want to avoid anything that has more than a minimal risk of causing you a large permanent loss.

Your investment strategy should also make use of both non-taxable qualified retirement plan accounts and taxable investment accounts, and consider which investments should be held in which accounts. Returns earned on money invested in qualified retirement accounts are not taxed until you withdraw the money in retirement. Returns earned on investments in a taxable investment account are taxed in the year they are earned. Your advisor should make sure your investments are held in the proper account to minimize your overall taxes.

Special Planning Considerations of Athletes and Other Celebrities

It is well understood in the financial advisory world that professional athletes have a unique challenge in that they have a short, and sometimes unpredictable, period to earn good money followed by a long retirement where they will likely need to live off their savings, at least partially.   This is pretty much the direct opposite of most of the population who work, earn and save for a long period then have a relatively short retirement period where they live off their savings.

Majority of the Population

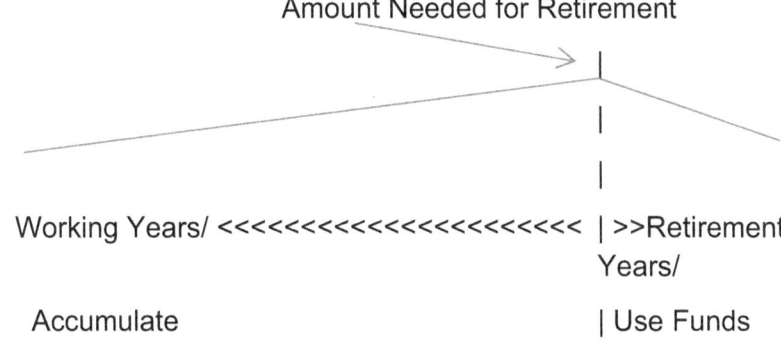

Amount Needed for Retirement

Working Years/ <<<<<<<<<<<<<<<<<<<<<<< | >>Retirement Years/

Accumulate | Use Funds

As shown above, the majority of people only make enough to be able to invest a little each year. As a result, the earnings, or returns, on their investments aren't large, especially in the early years; so it takes them a long time to accumulate the amount they need to retire.   Since they don't retire until they are 65 or 70, their retirement money only has to last for a relatively small number of years.

Typical Professional Athletes

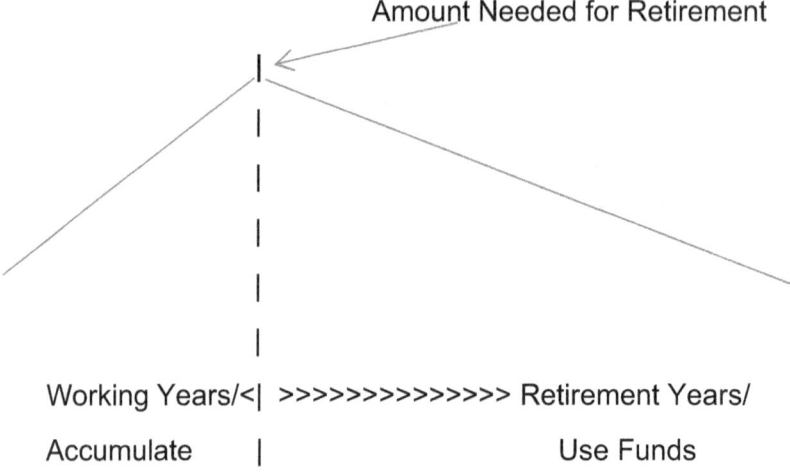

Amount Needed for Retirement

Working Years/<| >>>>>>>>>>>>>> Retirement Years/

Accumulate　　　|　　　　　　　　　Use Funds

In the case of professional athletes, many have the opportunity to accumulate enough wealth during a short playing career to last the rest of their lifetime. As mentioned above, the key is not in going after the highest possible returns on your investments; *the key is saving and investing enough out of your salary and other earnings each year and earning something around the overall market returns each year.* If you don't save enough each year, figuring you can make up for it by achieving returns that are far above average on future investments, you are mistaken and certainly won't live the comfortable life that you could.

Assuming that you do save enough each year, most financial advisors would agree that preservation of that wealth is the key to your future financial security (remember the First Rule: Don't Lose). Preservation means that the investment strategy should be low risk.

Many athletes who have lost big have instructed their advisors that they wanted their money put in safe, conservative investments but found out later that they were put in the riskiest, most unsuitable investments you could imagine. **Knowing what is and isn't risky will be important along with verifying that what you have been told has actually been done.**

Estate Planning

Estate Planning involves how to transfer your wealth to your spouse, children and others in ways that allow you to meet your objectives, while minimizing the taxes that will be paid. These transfers may take place while you are alive or at the time of your death.

It is important to undertake estate planning early in order to identify any conditions that need to be corrected to allow the most effective estate planning techniques to be used. These conditions can take some time to correct. For example, a married couple living in the U.S. where one spouse is an American citizen and one is not can have very costly consequences when you die. Correcting the situation can take some time so better to do it now rather than later. If you decide that you don't want to make the changes, at least it will be made with an understanding of the likely consequences.

Asset Protection Planning

Asset Protection is effectively part of Estate Planning, but it can be done without an Estate Plan. Asset Protection planning involves using trusts to hold legal ownership of your assets in such a way that they are protected from possible future liabilities, such as lawsuits, divorce and creditors.

It is important that your asset protection planning be undertaken before you are subject to potential claims from creditors. If a lawsuit has already been threatened, structuring your assets to try to protect them from the lawsuit generally won't protect them from that creditor if the lawsuit is successful.

Holding Your Investments

One issue that is overlooked by some advisors is how you take ownership of your investments. This is about whether you own your investments in your name or set up a trust or company to own them. This should ideally be part of your estate and asset protection planning. If not at least consider the following:

- If the investment is in publicly traded stocks and bonds, they can be held in your name without creating additional risk to you. The question that follows is whether they should be held in a tax advantaged account or in a taxable account.
- If the investment is in real estate, other hard assets or an operating business that could potentially cause harm to anyone, holding it in a company or possibly a trust should help to shield you from personal lawsuits.

Check with your advisory team.

....

....

Jaret Wright – Avoidable Losses Case #5

Jaret Wright was a very successful MLB pitcher. In 2013 he filed a lawsuit for $7.5 million against his advisors, including Todd LaRocca, CSI Capital Management Inc. ("CSI"), Taylor & Faust, and Sun Trust Bank Inc. According to the lawsuit, Wright engaged LaRocca as his investment advisor and money manager in 1998. At the time, LaRocca was associated with CSI.

Wright had apparently instructed LaRocca that he wanted to follow a conservative investment strategy but gave him discretionary authority to make investment decisions. Instead of conservative safe investments, LaRocca allegedly invested Wright's money in very risky illiquid real estate funds, and high risk alternative investments. Wright's lawsuit also claims that LaRocca and CSI required him to use Taylor & Faust for accounting and/or taxes, which effectively limited others' access to his financial records.

It is alleged that many of the investments LaRocca invested Wright's money in were not only high risk and illiquid; they also paid high commissions to LaRocca and CSI. Other investments were said to be managed or controlled by people LaRocca had a personal relationship with and who allegedly paid him undisclosed commissions.

What are some of the characteristics in Wright's case that are also commonly found in other cases?

- Although Wright wanted conservative investments he appears to have trusted what LaRocca told him, without doing any independent verification. Remember, trust but verify first. Understand what you are investing in. If you say you want conservative investments, you need proof of what you are investing in so you can know whether it is conservative or not.
- Wright's lawsuit alleges he was required to use Taylor & Faust. This put two related firms in a position to control access to his financial records. You don't want one firm to have access to your money and also do your accounting. Nor do you ever want to be told by an advisor that you have to use another service provider, whether they are related or not.
- According to the lawsuit, Wright had never been asked to complete standard risk profiles and other standard documents; nor had LaRocca completed written investment objectives. This is an illustration of why you should perform due diligence not only on the advisor but also on the firm he works for. Investment advisory firms are supposed to supervise their representatives and the investments they put their clients' money in. That includes ensuring appropriate information is gathered to know that the investments are suitable. But you can't take that for granted.
- As described in the lawsuit, the investments were neither suitable nor diversified. Suitability depends on an evaluation of your goals, other assets and income, and risk tolerance. If your advisor doesn't even go through these areas you should suspect that your investments may not be suitable. Get an independent opinion. And every financial advisor should automatically ensure you are diversified. If you see only a few large investments, be concerned and ask for an explanation, then get an independent assessment.

....

....

Summary

A personal financial plan is your financial playbook. Your financial advisor should have gone through the process of gathering information from you and working with you to prepare your personal financial plan, and should update it at least annually.

It is very important to understand that **the most important factor in determining how well off you and your family will be after you retire is how much you save each year** (assuming you avoid losing your savings and investments). If you don't save while you are earning, there is no investment that will make up for that at the end.

In addition to your personal financial plan, you should discuss with your advisor potential estate and asset protection planning. It may not be necessary now but going through the process may identify issues you didn't know were concerns.

Part VII – Other Issues and Risks

There are numerous other issues and risks, some of which are commented on below. Remember, the risks you face depend on many factors in your unique situation. The following sections may not include all of the issues and other risks you may face in your particular situation.

You Receive a Lot Less Than You Make

A million dollar (or even ten million for that matter) salary doesn't go as far as it used to.

Using very broad estimates, from a one million dollar salary, you won't take home even half that. Here is what it might look like:

Gross	$1,000,000
Less:	
Taxes withheld – Federal (say 40%)	(400,000)
Taxes withheld – State (say 10%)	(100,000)
Agent's commission (say 5%)	(50,000)
Other financial management fees (say 5%)	(50,000)
Net cash remaining – for the year	$400,000
Per month spread over 12 months	$33,333

For most people, $33,333 per month would pay all their expenses and leave some money for investing. The caveat is if you don't watch your expenses, including rent or mortgage payments, repaying loans, entertaining, and paying expenses for friends or relatives, it can go very quickly. That's why you need to pay attention to and manage your cash inflows and outflows.

Cash Management

Cash management is a very important element of meeting your financial goals. It helps ensure that you have funds available to meet daily needs as well as unanticipated emergencies, you're allocating your funds to the best uses including savings and investments, and you have control over your funds.

Cash management involves receiving and depositing your money and making sure it is managed appropriately. This means ensuring there is cash available as needed and that money that is not needed is invested so it is earning interest. One issue faced by many is that your annual income is not received evenly over the entire year. This may leave you with a period of some months where you have no money coming in. If you haven't planned, and put aside money for those months, you could find yourself having to borrow against your future earnings. It's okay to borrow to make a purchase such as a house, but borrowing to pay normal living expenses is a sure sign of a developing problem.

As stated above, if it's your agent or advisor who receives your earnings, they should be depositing them directly into an account set up only for your money so that it doesn't become mixed, or comingled, with other clients' money or with the agent or advisory firm's money. If your money is comingled in someone else's account, that money is at much greater risk than if it is in an account in your name.

Money that is going to be in a checking account to be used to cover your expenses should be sufficient to cover budgeted amounts for two or three months at most.

You should also have a contingency fund in case your income is interrupted. A contingency fund should have enough money in it to cover at least six months budgeted expenses and be kept in a bank account that would be available under emergency circumstances. These funds should be kept in a different financial institution than your primary bank to reduce the risk that you could lose access to everything at the same time. This happened to several MLB players who had all of their accounts and credit cards at Stanford Financial. Stanford was found to be a fraud and all accounts and investments at the institution were frozen for some time. Some players found they couldn't get cash to pay bills or even use their credit cards. Having your contingency account at another institution would have avoided that.

Budgeting

A budget is a necessary control mechanism for your finances. Even if you feel you can't live by a budget, you should have one as a control so that you can track how your money is being earned, spent and saved compared to what was expected. The budget should include information such as:

- The amounts you expect to receive monthly from each of your sources of income, for example
  - Salary;
  - Bonuses;
  - Endorsements;
  - Appearance fees;
  - Investment income;
  - Other
- The monthly payments you expect to make such as
  - Agent fees and expenses;
  - Other commissions;
  - Rent or mortgage payments and other living expenses;
  - Fees paid to your advisors;
  - Business expenses;
  - Personal expenses;
  - Income taxes; and
  - Additions to savings and investments.

Taxes

Income taxes must be paid on the amount you earned during a year less personal exemptions and allowable deductions. Many players have found themselves with large unpaid tax bills, mostly as a result of

- Under reporting income;
- Overstating allowable expenses; or
- Taxes being withheld from the player's salary or other earnings by the agent/advisor but not paid to the IRS.

The above actions are sometimes done by the player, or with the player's knowledge, but it seems more often it happens without their awareness. If you are knowingly participating in filing false tax returns, it's a bad move. Even Al Capone learned that.

Some people may suggest that investing offshore or just moving money offshore is a way to beat the IRS. **If you do have income from any source outside the U.S., it has to be reported.** If it is suggested that you can avoid taxes by sending the money outside the U.S., get a new advisor; otherwise you'll soon need a good lawyer. There are legitimate ways to manage your taxes, to an extent. A good tax advisor is a necessity to identify the best legitimate ways to minimize the taxes you pay.

The last thing to mention here is the danger of investing in anything simply because it will save you taxes. Over the years, there have been many investments have been sold to high income earners with the promise of reducing taxes by as much or more than the cost of the investment. These investments are sold as *tax shelters*. In past years, some have been successful but many others have been found to be illegal, and the lawyers and accountants who designed and sold them have gone to prison. The investors then had to pay taxes, penalties and interest, and they lost the money they originally invested because the investment had no real value outside the (disallowed) tax break. If an investment doesn't have value outside of tax reduction, steer clear.

Accounting

As mentioned above, your accounting should be done by a firm that is separate and independent from any advisors who have access to your funds or investments.

Your accountant's job is not to handle your money but is to record what is done with it, and prepare reports detailing what was done with your money, including

- the money you earn,
- the expenses you pay to make your living,
- expenses paid by your advisors on your behalf,

- expenses paid by credit card,
- the things purchased with your money,
- taxes withheld and paid to the IRS,
- loans taken out and loan payments, including interest,
- purchases or sales of investments, including interest or dividends received, and
- transfers between bank and/or investment accounts.

Your accounting records are used to record, summarize and report what happened with your earnings and other money. These records have two very important purposes. The first is to allow you to see what has happened to your finances over time (and ensure it wasn't being stolen or misused). The second use is to prepare your income taxes.

For both of the above purposes the accounting system needs to capture every transaction (receipts and expenses) in detail. As an example, if you have an entourage, what records are needed?

- Who was paid, what for and how much?
- Are payments to entourage members for salary or are they contractors?
- What are their expenses and are they tax deductible?
- If payments to them are tax deductible as salaries, appropriate deductions have to be made and recorded.
- If the payments aren't for services, are they gifts, and if so do they meet levels at which they have to be reported as gifts for tax purposes?

If you aren't tracking the use of your money in detail, it would be very easy for someone to tell you your money is going to the entourage but how would you ever know?

Accounting firms are often ranked as highly trusted among professions and businesses, but trusting anyone who has access to your money is dangerous, as you will see in the Patricia Cornwell case below. **If you value your wealth, make sure that whoever is doing your accounting does not have access to your money**

or investments. All they should be doing is recording it accurately in the accounting records and possibly preparing your taxes.

Mobile Devices, Computers and Security

The security of your personal and financial information is at risk almost any time you use your mobile device or computer. The topic of how to secure your information is beyond the scope of this book; but it is definitely important and should not be ignored.

Access to Your Wealth

Access to your wealth includes, but is not limited to, such things as:

- ability to direct where your money goes,
- receiving your salary or other income,
- paying your bills,
- being able to sign checks or make transfers from your accounts,
- holding your funds in their account,
- having a credit card on your account,
- borrowing money in your name,
- putting title of assets in their name;
- making, holding or selling investments on your behalf,
- being trustee of a trust that is for your or your family's benefit,
- being a signing officer of a company you own, or
- having a Power of Attorney over any aspect of your finances.

As mentioned above, the second category of fraud involves your advisor embezzling or diverting your money to some unsuitable or unintended purpose. Preferably you don't give them access, or at least limit how much of your wealth they can access. On the other hand, even if you try, you might not always realize that you are giving them access. For example, consider the following:

As mentioned earlier in the discussion of Antoine Walker's situation, an unlimited **Power of Attorney** ("POA") is a document that gives the person receiving it (the "Attorney in Fact") unlimited powers to do or sign or authorize anything you could do in your name. The Attorney in Fact can buy or sell property, take out loans or enter into contracts in your name. In contrast to the unlimited POA, you can give someone a limited POA to allow them to do some specified actions for a limited period of time. In Antoine Walker's situation, with his advisor having an unlimited POA and Walker not paying attention to his finances, his advisor could have bought and sold properties, and obtained mortgage loans without Walker ever knowing.

A noteworthy case of abuse of POAs involved advisors Phil Kenner and Tommy Constantine. Beginning in 2003, Kenner convinced close to 20 of his NHL clients to invest in a real estate development in Hawaii. To fund the development he arranged for the players to obtain loans in the form of lines of credit from Northern Trust. The players were required to provide other investments in stocks and bonds that they owned as security to the bank for the loans. They reportedly each gave a POA to Kenner, although he told them that he would not draw on their lines of credit or only do so with their permission. For almost every line of credit, a letter supposedly signed by the players authorized Northern Trust Bank to allow Kenner to access the line of credit to make direct transfers of money to one of his corporate accounts. To prevent the players from learning the balance of their lines of credit, Kenner arranged to have Northern Trust mail the statements for the lines of credit only to him, at his home in Scottsdale, Arizona.

In 2009, without warning, the bank sold the security (collateral) that the players had provided for the loans because of missed payments by Kenner. The lines of credit had been used by Kenner for personal expenses and to make other personal investments. Prosecutors say Kenner stole as much as $30 million from then current and retired NHL players who included Joe Juneau, Michael Peca, Bryan Berard, Darryl Sydor, Bill Ranford, Sergei Gonchar, Owen Nolan, Ethan Moreau, Jozef Stumpel and Jay McKee. In June 2015 Kenner and Constantine were found guilty of criminal charges.

When you give a financial advisor **discretionary authority** over your investment account, you are giving them the authority to invest your money as they see fit. There is nothing (other than the law) to stop the advisor from investing your money in anything, legitimate or not. And many times when the advisor misuses his discretionary authority by making improper investments, it's never detected. It's not advisable to give your advisor discretionary authority but if you do, make sure you are required to be advised before any investment is made.

Another more obvious scam involves your advisor offering you an investment opportunity and instructing you to **make your check to him personally**. This should never happen and if you get that request, you should immediately know something is wrong. Once you make a check out to your advisor you don't have any idea where the money is actually going.

Another way people sometimes give unintentional access to their money occurs when dealing with a smaller broker-dealer. Many small broker-dealers are owned by one or two people, who also own a related custodian (which holds purchased investments and does the record keeping for those investments). When you **make out your check or transfer money to the related custodian**, you have effectively given the broker-dealer owner access to your funds, potentially without knowing it is related and under their control.

Similarly, when you invest in a private company or other private investment, you are essentially handing your money over without any ability to really know if it's being used legitimately or wisely. That's because they can tell you whatever they want and you likely won't have any visibility to see whether it's true.

....
....

Patricia Cornwell was and continues to be a successful author of the Scarletta mystery/detective series. Her financial affairs and those of her company CEI were being managed by her own employees in what is called a family office. However, she was persuaded to transfer the management of all of her finances to Anchin, Block and Anchin ("Anchin"), a highly-regarded New York accounting firm. According to the civil claim she later filed against Anchin;

- Anchin became Ms. Cornwell's full service concierge business manager and then assumed responsibility for her accounting, investments and all other aspects of her business affairs. By 2006, an Anchin partner held full Powers of Attorney for CEI, Ms. Cornwell, and Ms. Cornwell's mother.

- All of CEI and Ms. Cornwell's incoming revenues, including investment income, went directly to Anchin. They opened multiple bank accounts, deposited the revenues, moved money between accounts, paid all expenses from the accounts and received the bank statements directly from the bank.

- Anchin issued invoices for their services monthly and authorized payment to themselves, charging upwards of $100,000 some months, without Ms. Cornwell knowing what she was being charged.

- She did not receive bank statements from her banks or passwords that would allow her to access her bank accounts online. Similarly, she did not regularly receive reports of investment balances or details of how her funds were invested or financial statements showing her net worth.

- Anchin had also borrowed several million dollars in her name but without her knowledge, comprised of mortgages for properties and a loan for the purchase of a helicopter.

After four years of Anchin handling her finances, Ms. Cornwell saw that her wealth had either not or barely increased, despite having made $89 million over that period. As reported in the Boston Globe,

---

Author Patricia Cornwell awarded $50.9m in suit

A federal court jury had just awarded her $50.9 million in damages, finding her former financial company cheated her, her wife, and her company out of tens of millions of dollars....

"For more than 90 years, the professionals at Anchin have built a reputation for honesty and integrity," the statement said. "The firm will endure despite today's outcome."

But one juror said that the company should take the jury's verdict as a call for more responsibility.

"I think at the end of the day, we came up with a fair decision, and hopefully Anchin will learn something," said John Martus, the foreman.... [25]

Despite winning the jury verdict, parts of the verdict and award were subsequently reversed and Ms. Cornwell has recently said she will not appeal. Even so, it's worth exploring the issues and what could have been done to avoid these problems.

Avoidable Losses?

A major issue illustrated in Patricia Cornwell's situation is the risk of allowing one firm, even a respected accounting firm, to look after all of your financial affairs; including

- Setting up bank accounts and having signing authority,
- Receiving and depositing her income,
- Paying her bills,
- Purchasing and selling investments,
- Making decisions about buying and leasing real estate,
- Arranging loans in her name;
- Doing her accounting, and
- Preparing and filing her taxes.

This full-service model allows an advisor to make decisions and carry them out, including moving money around and investing in anything they decide; then recording the transactions in the accounting records however they wish (whether correctly or not); and preparing your taxes without any other firm looking over your records. Do not let this happen to you.

There were some big red flags in the way Ms. Cornwell's affairs were allegedly being managed:

- Ms. Cornwell says she didn't receive bank statements or investment statements directly from the bank and wasn't given a password to allow her to look online at her accounts.
- She also didn't get regular reports of her transactions and net worth. Apparently even though these were requested, they weren't provided. Any withholding of information should be reason for immediately firing your financial managers or advisors.
- She wasn't receiving monthly invoices from Anchin outlining the amount they were charging her, let alone the details. Whenever a firm is providing services and is issuing and approving the invoices and signing checks to pay them without informing you, you shouldn't stand for it. Any time a firm can decide what services to provide to you and what hours are okay to charge you, you or your representative had better be approving those bills before they are being paid.
- Cornwell also apparently didn't know that Anchin had taken out millions of dollars in loans in her name. This shouldn't be tolerated without your prior authorization. In this case, it is likely that the loans were obtained using the Power of Attorney Cornwell had given to Anchin. Powers of Attorney should only be given for specified purposes and any use of them should be reported to you.

This case illustrates how important it is to be able to see clearly what is happening with your money. Although the specific losses were not identified or quantified, a client should always be fully informed about what has happened with their money. When those handling your finances have complete control of your finances and aren't providing regular reports, they know that no one is monitoring what they're doing. There is no reason you should ever be kept in the dark.

....

....

Bank Account Risks

Fraudulent Checks Written on Your Bank Account

The use of checks to make payments has been in decline for years. However, the 2016 Association of Financial Professionals' Payments Fraud and Control Survey notes that checks are still the most common method of fraudulent payment from a bank account.

Probably the main reason for this in many small and mid-size firms is that one person controls the unused checks, writes the checks, records the checks in the accounting records, receives the bank statements from the bank, prepares the bank reconciliation and prepares the financial reports that go to management. In this case, it doesn't matter if that person is authorized to sign the checks because only in very, very rare cases does anyone at the bank look at the signature on a check. Checks are processed electronically by banks without any person involved.

The risk of one person controlling the entire check payment process can be offset somewhat when there is close supervision and by having the bank statements received and reviewed by the owner or some other person. Unfortunately, this does not appear to happen very often.

The typical embezzlement by fraudulent check is quite simple. The bookkeeper writes a check to him or herself, forges the signature, records it in the accounting records as being paid to someone else, then if the cancelled check comes back, destroys the check. Now, banks generally don't return cancelled checks anyway and no-one seems to go online to compare the checks recorded to the checks that were actually processed by the banks. If your advisor is handling your finances and has opened one or more bank accounts for your money, make sure that you or your representative goes online and looks at every check (or electronic payment or withdrawal) paid from those accounts.

Here is an example of why this is important:

- Brian Ourand was SFX Financial Advisory Management Enterprises, Inc.'s President. According to the SEC Cease and Desist order,

> "From 2006 to 2011, Ourand misappropriated at least $670,000 from clients. During this time, Ourand wrote unauthorized checks from client bank accounts payable to cash or himself and wired unauthorized amounts to himself for his own personal use. He also wired money using client credit cards for unauthorized amounts to others for their personal use. In addition, Ourand forged a client's name and engaged in other deceptive conduct."

Wire Transfer Fraud and Spoofing

Wire transfer fraud has become much more frequent in the last couple of years. Generally it happens when a hacker gains access to your email account and password. With these, the hacker sends an email from your email account (this is called spoofing) to your financial advisor requesting money to be transferred to another bank account. When this happens, it usually takes some time afterwards to figure out that the email was fraudulent, and the money transferred is long gone.   To make matters worse, these are sometimes committed by or in collusion with an employee(s) of the financial advisory firm.

Credit Cards

You should not allow your agent or advisors to have credit cards on your accounts.   Instead, if they are paying expenses on your behalf, require that they submit a detailed invoice or expense report and reimburse them. Otherwise, without close review, it is too easy to charge their personal expenses or other clients' expenses or even to take cash advances from your account. At least if they must detail the expenses for reimbursement, it is easier to see what they are charging you for, as compared to trying to figure out from the limited information on a credit card statement.

Bill Pay Service

With busy schedules and being on the road, having a Bill Pay service manage and pay your bills can make sense. However, there have been numerous sizeable thefts of funds from these accounts.

The worst losses suffered from Bill Pay accounts involved financial advisor Jeff Rubin and his firm Pro Sports Financial ("PSF"). According the civil lawsuit filed against Rubin and PSF by about 20 current and former NFL players, Rubin set up Bill Pay accounts at a bank for each player. The Complaint states that Rubin then transferred funds from their bill pay accounts to other accounts without authorization. The largest amount taken from one of the player's account was $5.8 million and several lost $3 million or more.

How could such large losses occur from Bill Pay accounts? Generally these accounts should only have enough money to cover 2 – 3 months' worth of bills, at most, and the maximum balance in the accounts will be restricted to a certain amount. However, what is often not restricted is how often money can be transferred into and out of the account. So even if the maximum amount of money held in the account at any point in time is restricted, that doesn't restrict how much can flow into and out of the account improperly. For example, if the maximum balance allowed in the Bill Pay account is $20,000 that won't stop $20,000 from being transferred into then out of the account each day.   This can add up to a big loss very quickly.

Loans – Authorization and Direction of Loan Proceeds

Many athletes' financial problems involve borrowing too much during their playing days, while they are making very good salaries. It appears that some of this may arise from poor cash management, including failing to plan for off season months when no pay checks are coming in. In other cases, it seems that players are encouraged to take out loans to make investments now rather than waiting until they could invest their own cash. In those cases, there's a good chance that the advisor is benefitting in some way from the transactions.

Another common problem involves the advisor arranging a loan for a player where the advisor has control of when money is advanced from the loan and where it is sent. While this might seem like a very convenient arrangement, it has often resulted in money being advanced to and used by the advisor, but the player still being responsible for repaying the loan. And this can happen without the player ever being aware (because the advisor uses the loan for his own benefit and then repays it using more of the player's money) unless the loan isn't repaid and the bank contacts you. For example,

- Vince Young sued his advisor Ronald Peoples claiming he defrauded him of $5.5 million and impersonated him to get a $700,000 loan. According to Young, he never received any of the loan proceeds. The suit was settled for an agreed $2 million judgment.
- Kareem Abdul-Jabbar sued his advisor, Tom Collins, for $59 million. Collins had authority to take out loans in Abdul-Jabbar's name, allegedly took out more than $9 million in loans and made risky investments without his knowledge.
- Jack Johnson turned over management of his finances to his parents. It has been reported that in addition to going through the money he has earned, they took out $15 million in loans at high interest rates, apparently without his knowledge.

If you have given your advisors authority to take out loans in your name (usually by giving them a Power of Attorney), which I wouldn't advise; make sure that the activity in your loan account is closely monitored, including how the money from the loan is used.

Debt and Contingent Liabilities

Debt is a very dangerous tool. It seems that too often it has to be repaid at the worst time, when you don't have the money to pay. As mentioned earlier, using margin or leverage involves borrowing to make investments, supposedly to allow you to earn more. If the investment loses value, you can end up losing all your investment and still have to repay the loan.

At least while you are busy with your career and aren't fully involved in managing your personal finances, don't go into debt. If Antoine Walker had waited until he could buy each apartment without debt, he would have avoided bankruptcy.

A debt is also called a liability. Contingent liabilities are debts that you could end up having to repay. The most common occurrence is when a company you own takes out a loan and you are asked to provide your personal guarantee that the loan will be repaid. If the company goes bankrupt and can't pay the loan back, you will have to pay it with your personal money unless you also are bankrupt.

A similar occurrence involves helping a family member or friend to get a loan by guaranteeing the loan. More often than you would think, the person whose loan you guaranteed doesn't repay it and the guarantor (you) has to repay it. Do not guarantee any loan or other debt for anyone unless you are truly prepared to pay it off.

Other Earnings

As professional athletes or entertainers you probably don't receive all your income in a regular monthly paycheck. Even if you are receiving a regular paycheck as your main source of income, it's quite likely that you also have other, less regular sources. These might include bonuses, profit participation, royalties, appearance fees, endorsements, sponsorships, licensing fees, or distributions from business ventures.

With these non-paycheck irregular earnings, the amounts of payments vary, making it difficult to know whether you are receiving the complete amount you are entitled to. First, the gross amount of your earnings before taxes or other deductions may vary widely. Then there can be other deductions, potentially including expenses of earning the income, commissions, and other deductions. Also, there are income taxes being deducted which also can vary depending upon the state or states where the money was earned. **The point is that since it is difficult to know what you should be receiving, it is very easy for some of your earnings to be skimmed off and diverted to someone else.**

It is important to ensure that you have a written contract with the company you are doing work for or partnering with that covers exactly how your earnings are to be determined and what expenses will be deducted. You should request that whoever is paying you also directly sends you a statement of earnings, amounts deducted and net amount paid to you. Periodically you should have an independent party audit your earnings from these other sources to ensure that you are receiving all that you are entitled to.

If you watched the movie *Straight Outta Compton*, you saw Paul Giamatti as the agent living large while the band worked endlessly with little to show for it. It's a great example of what happens if no one is watching. First make sure the contract protects you and then that the money is being handled as the contract directs.

Insurance

Insurance provides financial protection against certain losses you could suffer. In basic terms, you pay the insurance company and in return, if you do suffer a loss, they pay you the amount you lost. The amount you pay the insurance company, called premiums, is much less than the maximum amount of loss you are insured for, but the insurance company counts on the fact that most insured losses will not actually occur so they keep the premiums. By buying insurance you are paying out some known amount to protect you from the chance of suffering a much larger loss.

Insurance is available to guard against loss of income, loss of a home or car, loss from a lawsuit judgment, from crime and many other risks. For some of these risks, it's better to take precautions against them happening but for others buying insurance is the only real way to reduce the risk of loss. It's surprising, when you start thinking about it, just how many things can cause losses.

Unfortunately when it comes to your investments, there is no insurance available against the value of your investments going down.

If you have invested through a broker-dealer or fund manager that is insured by SIPC ("Securities Investor Protection Corporation"), you are insured for up to $500,000 if the broker-dealer goes out of business **and the investments in your brokerage accounts are missing**. You really can't get insurance to protect you against investing in fraudulent investments.

Life and Disability Insurance

Life insurance will provide money to your family or other person(s) you designate if you die with the policy in force. Insurance is also available to guard against loss of income from injury (disability insurance). These can both be good products but as with any other investment, be careful. Make sure you know what coverage is in place through your players' association and under what conditions it will pay out before agreeing to pay for additional disability or life insurance. The people selling you insurance are making big commissions from the insurance companies and may try to sell you far more coverage than you need.

Here are a couple of examples of alleged insurance scams:

- o Billy Crafton was Brent Celek's financial advisor. Shortly after Celek received a big contract, Crafton recommended Celek obtain a universal life insurance policy which required a premium payment of

$1,200,000. Unknown to Celek, this life insurance investment recommended by Crafton was a scheme created by him to generate revenue for the insurance agent, who kicked-back part of the commission to Crafton.

- o Eva Weinberg and her brother sold Dwight Freeney life insurance policies totaling $55 million. These paid commissions of $450,000 to Weinberg. The policies required annual payments of $510,000 for 15 years; something Freeney very likely would not be able to continue to make.
- o Insurance broker Jerry Goldman deliberately overcharged Tom Hanks, Andy Summers and others by $800,000 on insurance policies.
- o In some cases, the money paid for the policy has been pocketed and no policy was ever issued.

Philanthropy

Many successful people want to give back, to help people overcome the challenges they face or to leave a legacy. They also, rightfully, are happy to take the tax breaks available when giving to charitable foundations. One way to accomplish their goals and obtain a tax break is to set up their own charitable foundation, and donate their own money, and reduce their income taxes.

Unfortunately having good intentions does not mean that your money inside a charitable foundation will be any less exposed to the risks of embezzlement or fraud than when it is in your personal bank account. The person who manages the foundation and its money and other assets needs to be researched the same as any other financial advisor or manager. And the money and investments held by the foundation need to be monitored by you or your representative who does not have access to those assets, just as with your personal bank and investment accounts.

Non-Investment Risks

It is obvious from the earlier mentioned cases that the biggest risks to your money and future financial security are connected to your **advisors**, **investments** and **cash management**, but there are other sources of risk that can also lead to major losses, such as:

- Associates;
- Cybercrime;
- Healthcare;
- Household employees;
- Use of information technology and social media;
- ID Theft;
- Injury;
- Lawsuits;
- Catastrophic disasters; and
- Outside business or charitable activities.

Some of the above risk areas don't receive as much attention as others but they can all cause or lead to significant losses of your wealth and financial security. Although I am not going into these, you should be aware of them and assess the extent of the risk they represent to you.

Your Role

It's your money and your financial security you're trying to keep. You owe it to yourself and your family to treat its preservation seriously. Don't just hand over your money to the advisor who tells you he will get you the highest return.

Below I've restated some observations that will help to decrease your risks.

Risky Behavior

- Don't

- give your advisor an unlimited Power of Attorney or authorization, always limit it to what needs to be done;
- have your advisor act as executor or trustee for you;
- sign blank or partially completed documents;
- allow the advisor to share ownership or be the beneficiary of any investment, insurance policy, trust or anything else;
- allow the primary mailing address on a bank or investment account be the advisor's address;
- make checks out to your advisor when making an investment;
- provide loans or loan guarantees to your advisor;
- respond to any pressure to invest;
- give your advisor discretionary authority over your investments and investment accounts.

- Don't invest in opportunities that are
  - Unregistered;
  - Exempt from registration (unless it's money you can afford to lose and you have done in depth research);
  - Hot tips;
  - No risk investments;
  - Guaranteed not to lose;
  - Urgent; invest now or lose out on the chance;
  - Based on inside tips;
  - Only available to an exclusive group;
  - Only set up for tax purposes.
- Don't have unrealistic expectations and insist on beating the market.

- Don't make decisions based on *short term results.*

- Don't decide to invest simply because the investment has the highest rate of return.

- Don't rely on an investment's past performance; it doesn't predict future performance.

Summary

It's your money and your financial security you're trying to preserve. You owe it to yourself and your family to treat its preservation seriously. In addition to losses that may occur from investing, there are numerous other areas where your wealth can be put at risk. It's particularly important to know who has access to your wealth and be alert to how you can be put at risk in these other areas.

Part VIII – Monitoring – Watching Out For Avoidable Losses

According to an FBI statement of facts, in one recorded call, Joseph Vaccaro of Dynasty Management explained to Billy Crafton that,

> "My big thing is, these guys would all fuck us in a heartbeat if they could. So if I'm going to have a player, I'm going to make as much money as I can make because I run the risk of him firing me at any time for no reason."

Wow! If this is your advisor's attitude, someone better be watching.

For me, one of the most interesting aspects of watching Antoine Walker's interview by Stephen A Smith (October, 2012) was his answer when asked, "So Antoine, are you saying you mostly blame the financial advisors who put you in the real estate deals to begin with?" Walker's response was that *"I don't blame the advisors, I more so blame myself"*. He later added, "By me not being able to watch everything, … and unaware of all the things going on, you know it makes it very tough to manage, so that's one thing, so I'm more mad at myself, more so than I am at my financial advisor…" Later he added,

> "If you're not there to watch it bad things are going to happen." [26]

That's as true a statement as you'll hear from anyone. Martina Navratilova gets it.

Auditor watches Martina's money managers

By Liz Mullen, Staff Writer

Martina Navratilova has some financial advice for her fellow athletes:

> "Whoever is handling your money, you need someone else to audit your money," said Navratilova, who earned $20 million while winning more tournaments than any professional tennis player in history.
>
> Another piece of advice — "You need to get an opinion from someone with no agenda, and most people around athletes have an agenda," she said. [27]

When you hire a financial advisory firm to manage your financial affairs, you probably have an expectation that they will watch over your finances and look out for risks or problems. But unless it's specified in writing in your agreement with the firm, it's not likely happening.

But more importantly, even if it is written in your agreement, your advisory firm still shouldn't be relied upon to provide assurance everything is okay. The reason is that if the firm either manages your finances or has access to your bank and investment accounts or makes financial decisions, then having them monitor your financial affairs means they are watching over their own decisions, responsibilities and actions. This clearly puts them in a conflict of interest. For example, if an employee of their firm did do something improper, such as "borrowing" money from your account, it's questionable whether they would report it to you. Or if your advisor uses some of your money for his personal expenses, he's not going to report that to you.

Make sure that the person watching your money is either you (if you are comfortable doing this) or your representative (someone independent from your advisors), who can't access your bank or investment accounts or make financial decisions; and doesn't have some other conflict of interest (for example, being another advisor who might want your business).

Here's how one journalist described the independence and monitoring issue:

Unsportsmanlike Conduct: The Exploitation of Black Athletes – Part II

In the typical scenario, a "qualified" agent lands a client and then quickly recommends a financial advisor. Or, vice versa. Maybe the pair recruits together. Maybe they just vouch for "their guy." Maybe there are kickbacks. Maybe there is the expectation of future swaps. However it goes down, in the end, a player thinks he has two sets of independent, trustworthy eyes on his money when, in fact, he has none. [28]

Monitoring your financial affairs requires that you, or your representative, are watching over the following:

- The activity in your bank and investment accounts;

- Whether your earnings are being deposited to your accounts;

- How your money is being used and where it's going;

- What investments are being bought and sold; and

- Whether the activity is consistent with what has been authorized and intended.

Monitoring should also include a monthly or quarterly review of what has happened in your accounts compared to your budget and financial plan. This review should cover your salary as well as other sources of monies received; what expenses, purchases and investments your money was used for (including advisory fees and expenses); and also your overall increase/decrease in your wealth. But keeping in mind previously mentioned cautions; the results need to be properly interpreted. In addition, the review should cover any new contracts, agreements, loans or other obligations entered into. And, of course, any changes in your life that could have an impact on your financial objectives need to be taken into account.

Gilbert Arenas – A Lesson about Independence and Monitoring

In a lawsuit filed in November 2015, NBA superstar Gilbert Arenas claimed he hired Boulevard Management ("Boulevard"), a well-known business management firm in Hollywood to manage and monitor his financial affairs. Apparently, while Boulevard was providing financial services Arenas hired a friend, John White, to provide personal non-financial services. However, on several occasions White, who allegedly did not have authority, directed Boulevard to transfer funds from one of Arenas' bank accounts to another. White then reportedly embezzled millions of dollars from that second bank account.

Arenas claims that he hired Boulevard to manage and monitor his finances and they were negligent. The following excerpt from the lawsuit describes Arenas' apparent expectations:

> "In October 2006, Arenas was referred to Knispel and Boulevard because of their reputation for providing guidance to high profile celebrities and professional athletes. Arenas met with Knispel and entered into an oral agreement with Knispel and Boulevard whereby Defendants would provide business and financial management services to Arenas. Boulevard agreed to provide Arenas the specialized services exactly as promoted in the press and its own website, including management of Arenas' bank accounts; management of Arenas' credit card accounts; payment of Arenas' expenses; providing sufficient cash for Arenas to pay his personal expenses; management of investment and retirement accounts; management of real estate investments; and provision of advice regarding wealth and cash management, growth, income preservation, and wise investment strategies. Boulevard was also tasked with managing several business entities formed by Arenas.

"Starting in October 2006, Boulevard took control of all of Arenas' business and personal accounts, which Boulevard was hired to monitor and manage for Arenas. Boulevard agreed to monitor Arenas' use of cash in order to protect Arenas' earnings to avoid the "financial disasters" that tend to flow from "unsound spending habits, poor management, or speculative financial advice" as once cautioned by Boulevard in its website.

"When he hired Boulevard, Arenas believed and intended that Knispel would use a system of checks and balances to supervise and monitor an established top tier team of advisors, bookkeepers and managers who would closely and competently monitor Arenas' financial affairs in order to protect his earnings."

What's wrong in this scenario?

- Let's start with hiring a firm because of their reputation. Just because a firm is well known and has famous clientele doesn't mean your wealth is safe. Don't assume that the others have done research or other due diligence on the firm. Remember Bernie Madoff and his wealthy and famous clientele? People invested because they felt others knew it was safe. Another example is the case of Kenneth Starr, a financial advisor to celebrities for 20 years before he was convicted of stealing $30 million from his clients, including Barbara Walters, Al Pacino, Annie Leibovitz, Ron Howard, Liam Neeson and many others. Your due diligence has to look deeper than the surface reputation. What processes do they actually have in place; how well screened and trained are employees, etc. And of course, what is really happening with the money, not just what is supposed to happen.
- Second, Boulevard Management was pretty well a full-service firm. It appears that if not actually performing the services, they were arranging and directing the services.

This means that if there is a problem, they are likely the only ones who would see it.

- Lastly, and very well illustrated by this situation, is that Arenas expected Boulevard to be monitoring the same activity that they were responsible for conducting. If there is one major lesson that every accountant knows, **it is that you should never have a person or firm monitoring their own activities. The monitor has to be either (1) you or (2) someone independent of those managing your wealth who can't access, move, direct or make decisions about your money, investments or other wealth AND doesn't have any other conflicts of interest.**

Another aspect of this lawsuit against Boulevard is also very instructive. The lawsuit states,

"In 2013, Boulevard asked attorney Dennis Roach ("Roach") to represent Arenas in the investigation of White's theft of Arenas' funds.

"Arenas is informed and believes and thereon alleges that Roach is counsel for Boulevard and Knispel on numerous matters. Roach is also close personal friends with Knispel.

"Roach failed to investigate all of the facts surrounding the theft of Arenas' funds, ignored Defendants' responsibility for the theft, and abdicated his ethical responsibility to zealously advocate for Arenas, and to give Arenas undivided loyalty in the pursuit of remedies arising from the theft of Arenas' funds.

"Instead, Roach focused entirely on protecting the Boulevard Defendants from their involvement in White's theft, hiring attorneys in Florida to pursue potential civil claims against White (which were never filed), and communicating with the U.S. Attorneys investigating the matter. These tasks were a diversion from, and in lieu of, Roach's ethical duty to simultaneously pursue remedies against all culpable parties - including Boulevard."

And further on the lawsuit says,

"Notably, the Florida civil attorneys hired by Roach communicated with Roach and Boulevard - not Arenas - in their pursuit of potential claims arising from the theft by White.

"Neither Roach, nor the Florida civil attorneys hired by Roach, ever warned Arenas that Boulevard shared legal responsibility for the theft by John White."

If you accept the above allegations, it appears that there was a clear conflict of interest at work here, although it might have looked to Arenas that Boulevard was taking care of him. Clearly if Boulevard was negligent, then they might be held responsible for at least some of the losses, resulting in a conflict for management between protecting Boulevard or protecting Arenas.

When you allow the same firm to manage your wealth and to monitor their own actions, you should be very concerned.

How Would You Know?

Let's assume you work with advisors who appear to be qualified and trustworthy. But if one of your advisors was somehow stealing from you, or defrauding you, or was scammed into investing your money in a fraudulent investment, do you think it would be discovered, and if so, how?

If someone did manage to get access to your assets and steal from you, how large of a loss would really hurt you? Does your advisor manage or have access to that amount?

Do you know if anyone is monitoring changes that might put you at risk? Keep in mind that new risks emerge and others evolve as new investment vehicles, technologies, and regulations are introduced.

If you were watching over your bank accounts, investments and financial management, do you feel confident that you would be likely to detect a problem? Or does it seem that your financial affairs are a black box that that you can't really understand?

Do you know who has signing authority on your bank and investment accounts? Are there limits on how much can be moved from your accounts? If these limits or signing authorities were changed, would you know?

A case was recently filed by the SEC against advisor Ash Narayan. Mark Sanchez, Mark Peavey and Roy Oswalt were allegedly defrauded of almost $30 million by Narayan, most of it through unauthorized transfers from their accounts to a company Narayan knew was in financial difficulty and in which he owned more than 3 million shares. Had their accounts been monitored, these unauthorized transactions would have been quickly identified and losses, if any, could have been minimized.

The Importance of Monitoring - Deterrence

The importance of monitoring your financial affairs can't be overstated. Why?

Monitoring means you represent a harder target for anyone wanting to embezzle or defraud you. It is widely known that most criminal enterprises don't pursue hard targets. If controls are in place, of which monitoring is one strong control, criminals will usually move on to a softer target. You will be too much work and they don't want to be caught.

There is no such thing as 100% assurance that all crimes or abuses of your finances will be stopped even with the best controls including monitoring. But the person considering your wealth as a target will see that it will take much more work to cover up what they are doing, to prevent being detected. And the more elaborate the cover up, the greater the chance of a slip up.

Criminals don't want to be caught. If the accounts are being watched, there is a greater chance of being caught than if there is no one watching. People who do steal or commit fraud don't want to be caught and generally won't take the chance if it's being watched.

The Importance of Monitoring – Early Detection

If your financial plan is going poorly, for example if you suffer large investment losses, it is always possible that your advisor would prefer not to explain clearly what really happened. He might hope that those losses would be recovered the next year and he doesn't lose you as a client; but many frauds have shown that that is a slippery slope of increasing losses.   Each time there are new losses, or the advisor is short of funds and borrows from you, it becomes much easier for him to justify his actions. History has shown small thefts, given time, will grow into large thefts.

Most frauds are not identified until the investor funds have been substantially lost. You need to know what is really happening with your wealth and not receive the cleaned up, misreported version.   Case in point:

Alanis Morissette Claims Ex-Business Manager Stole $4.7M

5/17/2016 by Ashley Cullins

Alanis Morissette was robbed of at least $4.7 million by her former business manager, according to a complaint filed Tuesday in Los Angeles County Superior Court.

The singer is suing Jonathan Schwartz and GSO Business Management for breach of fiduciary duty, conversion, fraud and negligence.

"Defendants concealed these distributions from Morissette, convincing her that she was in tremendous financial shape when, in fact, they were draining her assets and leading her on a road that could have led to financial ruin," states the complaint.

Schwartz handled Morissette's finances from 2009 to 2016 and was responsible for collecting income, managing investment accounts and paying bills on her behalf. According to the complaint, she fired him in March because he failed to respond in a timely manner to her requests for information about her finances.

As stated, this embezzlement took place over several years during which Schwartz provided advice, management and accounting without oversight.

Another recent case with similarities involved former Indianapolis Colt Cory Redding. He hired his financial advisor, Kenneth Ray Cleveland, in 2003 when he decided he needed financial advice. He was referred to Cleveland by a professor at the University of Texas. Cleveland apparently proposed investing in conservative fixed-income investments that would provide interest payments without depleting the principal, but by 2007 he had begun spending Redding's money.

From 2003 through 2015 Redding gave Cleveland $7 million to invest. In 2015 the fraud was uncovered when Redding wanted to withdraw his money but Cleveland couldn't produce it.

The fraud was able to continue for years because Cleveland managed Redding's investments and also did his accounting, so no one else saw what was actually going on. Cleveland provided Redding with forged account statements and paid him interest as expected. However, the interest was paid from the money Redding was handing over while Cleveland was spending the rest.

Clearly Redding trusted Cleveland. Cleveland was recommended to him, the investing strategy was conservative and he received the interest payments he expected. However there wasn't any independent custodian to confirm and hold the investments, or to confirm the source of the money he was receiving.

This was another case of the fraud continuing past the end of the player's career. When it was uncovered, it was too late for Redding to make up the losses. Had the part of his finances managed by Cleveland been monitored or periodically audited by a knowledgeable independent representative, it could have detected the fraud much sooner, thereby decreasing the amount of loss.

....

Unfortunately your money is a target. And there are many people who are, or with the right opportunity would be, quite happy to take as much of it as they can. I know this. But it's not just my word. Consider the following:

In July 2013 Labaton Sucharow, a well-respected New York law firm, released the results of their second annual U.S. Financial Services Industry Survey, entitled *Wall Street in Crisis: A Perfect Storm Looming*. The findings from the survey of financial professionals included the following:

- 52% felt it was likely that their competitors engaged in unethical or illegal activity;

- 23% had observed or had firsthand knowledge of wrongdoing in the workplace;

- 29% believed that financial services professionals may need to engage in unethical or illegal activity in order to be successful;

- 28% felt that the financial services industry did not put the interests of clients first.

This is astounding and frightening. I can't imagine any other profession where so many of its own members believe there is such a high level of unethical or illegal behavior.

Money may not buy happiness, but going from rich to poor won't make most people happier. If you lose your wealth, your life will change drastically – for the worse. Imagine if your advisor made a mistake and entrusted your wealth to the wrong person, not realizing that he had put your assets at risk. If no-one is monitoring, who would possibly know?

If you think that the Federal securities regulators are closely watching your advisors, and you can rely on them to protect you from investment related fraud, consider the following information from The Hill's Congress Blog by Heath Abshure dated August 7, 2013. It states:

"Currently, the SEC has resources only to examine approximately 8 percent of the roughly 11,000 federally registered investment advisors (IAs) nationwide.

"The average SEC-registered investment advisor is looked at by regulators only once every 10 to 13 years, and the frequency of SEC examinations of investment advisors has decreased 50 percent since 2004. Moreover, some 40 percent of advisors registered with the SEC, and nominally policed by the federal government, have, in fact, never been examined." [32]

Since the regulators don't have the resources to protect you, and you shouldn't count on your advisors to monitor or audit themselves, you really should be concerned if you aren't able to effectively monitor your own money and investments.

Questions I Wonder About

Besides my own experience investigating fraud and financial crimes, I have spent a considerable amount of time studying and researching fraud against individuals and families; but I still have many questions. I can't help but wonder:

- Why would any person pass over control of their wealth to someone without verifying their competence, character and financial well-being?
- Why would an advisor not make his client aware of his exact financial situation, good or bad, long before the client retires?
- Why would an advisor allow his client to spend out of control without making sure that he was aware that he was in terrible financial shape?

- When an athlete retires and is broke, why would other clients stay with that same advisor? The advisor certainly hasn't done a good job with the broke client.
- When an athlete is defrauded or financially abused by an advisor, why would other clients of the advisory firm not insist on an independent investigation of their accounts and transactions? Independent does not mean an investigation done internally by their people.
- Why don't players' associations require financial advisors to file annual financial statements including an accounting of the funds received from each player they manage?
- And why don't the players' associations randomly select financial advisors and examine their financial records specifically addressing risky or unethical/dishonest practices that could put clients' financial security at risk?

Summary

Martina Navratilova said it best, ""Whoever is handling your money, you need someone else to audit your money." Another good piece of advice from Navratilova: "You need to get an opinion from someone with no agenda, and most people around athletes have an agenda".

If you don't have the time or interest or knowledge to monitor your own financial affairs, you need your representative to do it on your behalf. That representative should be knowledgeable, shouldn't have any access to your funds, and should be independent of your advisors.

Monitoring has several benefits. People who embezzle or defraud others are far less likely to target those clients who monitor what is going on in their accounts. They don't want to be caught so they go after the easy targets. If there is embezzlement or fraud, or mismanagement, any problems are likely to be detected much sooner when monitored; and earlier detection means lower losses.

Although your advisor may not like the idea of someone monitoring how your finances are being managed, it shouldn't be about his preference. If all is being handled properly, more credit to him. And if something is putting you at risk, a good advisor would want to know so he can take corrective action. If an advisor objects, you would have to wonder why.

The objection that some advisors may raise is the added cost of monitoring if you hire someone to do it for you. Unfortunately all professional services come with a cost. It will be your decision whether the added comfort you get from hiring a monitor is worth the cost.   In the end, the cost will be small in comparison to becoming a victim of fraud, embezzlement, incompetence or bad judgment.

Part IX – Frequent Elements of Fraud Against Athletes and Celebrities

The following observations are identified from my personal experience, a review of articles, lawsuits, SEC documents and interviews. These are observations of high risk issues that appear frequently **(but not always)** in frauds against players, celebrities and other successful individuals:

Player/Celebrity Clients

- Hired their financial advisor without doing any background investigation or other due diligence procedures. Advisors often had prior client complaints or regulatory issues;

- Relied heavily on one advisor and allowed the advisor's firm to manage their money and investments and do their accounting;

- Trusted their advisors/managers with their money without monitoring or oversight or taking other steps to verify that the trust was deserved;

- Didn't get a second opinion on investment recommendations;

- Were not receiving their bank statements or their investment account statements directly from the bank or the custodians holding their investments and didn't have online access to view their account transactions;

- Gave their adviser an unlimited Power of Attorney ("POA") which allowed their advisor to do anything with their client's money or investments, or take out loans, in the client's name. If a POA is necessary, always limit it to only authorize specific transactions that need to be done and in a specific time period;

- Didn't know how much money and investments or debts they had, or how their money was being used;

- Felt like they were being kept in the dark;

Investment Advisors

- Known for their high profile and big lifestyle;
- Were heavy gamblers;
- Provided full service including investment advice, financial management and accounting;
- Was little or no oversight of advisor transactions and reporting;
- Misrepresented their professional status, clientele and investment returns;
- Were okay with client's free-spending and didn't encourage financial responsibility;
- Asked clients to sign documents with unanswered questions or incomplete information filled in;
- Moved from one firm to another or started their own firm and brought existing clients with them;
- Didn't try to educate clients about investing;
- Borrowed money from clients;
- Asked clients to co-sign or guarantee the advisor's loans from a bank or other party;
- Used registration with Players' Association to influence potential clients;

Investment Management

- Didn't diversify investments to reduce risk;
- Encouraged investing in higher risk private investments such as restaurants and start-up businesses, rather than lower risk publicly traded low cost mutual funds and Exchange Traded Funds;
- Put money in non-liquid investments that couldn't be sold or money withdrawn resulting in problems for the client when

unexpected need for cash arose, for example on division of assets in a divorce;

- Conducted unauthorized transactions in client bank or investment accounts;

- Took out loans in client's name;

- Invested client money in unsuitable or fraudulent investments;

- Invested client money in projects where the advisor had an ownership interest; often including real estate, restaurants, golf courses, etc.

- Recommended investments without doing any research or other due diligence on them;

- Received large commissions for making high risk investments with client money (in some cases these were kickbacks for knowingly investing in fraudulent investments);

- Churned client investment accounts. Churning refers to an advisor frequently buying and selling stocks in a client's investment account to earn higher commissions. This hasn't been a big cause of losses for athletes and celebrities because their money has not generally been invested in publicly traded stocks.

Investments

- Invested in high risk investments such as

  - Private placements of unregistered or exempt investments
  - Promissory Notes
  - Start-up businesses such as bars and restaurants
  - Property development projects
  - Commodities Trading Accounts
  - Foreign Exchange contracts ("FOREX")
  - Alternative investments

- Investments in latest high profile schemes – eg. Initial Coin Offerings
- Private placements of unregistered or exempt investments and promissory notes were the most common fraudulent investments;

- Used client money to purchase investments at inflated prices;

- Clients' money was generally given to the advisor for investment rather than to an independent custodian. This meant there was no independent party to confirm the money went where it was supposed to or that it was used as represented.

Insurance

- Agents/advisors often are licensed to sell insurance, which they sell to their own clients. If your agent/advisor is selling you insurance, this creates a conflict of interest because insurance pays high commissions to whoever sells you the policy. The question this conflict raises is whether you are getting the right insurance to meet your needs or the policy that pays the most to the advisor. The amount of commissions paid to the advisor for selling you a life insurance policy is often close to the amount you pay for the policy in the first year.

- Here's an example of an excessive life insurance policy. Billy Crafton, a financial advisor to many professional athletes, reportedly advised and led Kevin Correia to purchase a life insurance policy. The policy required annual payments of $608,846 for the next 10 years; with very large commissions to Crafton.

Cash Management

- Received and deposited client's income into advisor's or advisory firm's operating bank account then used the funds for operating his business;

- Skimmed money from client deposits, especially where the income varied over time or was collected in cash.

- Advisor withdrew cash from client bank accounts to give to clients for their daily spending or to pay members of the entourage, but also made unauthorized withdrawals for the advisor's personal use;

- Advisor transferred client money from or wrote checks on client bank accounts for his own benefit but recorded them as payments to known businesses;

- Advisor received and deposited money meant for investments in an account the advisor controlled, rather than the money being paid directly to an investment custodian. The money was stolen and used for personal purposes, not invested;

Credit Cards

- Used a credit card on client's account and charged personal expenses;

Loans

- Arranged loans for client and also directed when and where the loan proceeds were advanced, including to pay advisor's personal expenses;

- Loans were taken out in the client's name and used by the advisor, without the client being aware of the loan.

- Repaid advisor's personal loans from client accounts;

Power of Attorney

- Advisor requested an unlimited Power of Attorney;

- Forged client's signature on Power of Attorney

- Used the client's Power of Attorney for unauthorized personal purposes including taking out loans, buying and selling properties and cars, and entering contracts;

Purchases

- Sent clients to make purchases at businesses that overcharged client and kicked back the overcharges to the advisor;

- Purchased assets, often real estate, but puts title in advisor's name;

- Received kickbacks on purchases of real estate at inflated prices;

Bill Pay

- Paid Advisor's personal bills with client money;

- Set up and paid fake vendors;

- Transferred money into client bill-pay bank account but then transferred money to Advisor's own accounts or those of related parties;

Overcharges

- Billed clients for expenses that should be covered by the fees the client was charged. Your contract should set out clearly what expenses are covered by your fees and what other expenses you will be charged for;

- Charged clients undisclosed fees;

- Overcharged clients by double charging or by miscalculating the disclosed his fees.

Don't assume that the fees you are charged couldn't amount to much. A SEC Complaint dated August 22, 2017 against Jeremy Joseph Drake summarized how he overcharged his clients:

Drake told the Clients, a high-profile professional athlete and his spouse, that they were being charged a special, VIP rate of between 0.15% and 0.20% of their assets under management, when, in fact, they were being charged and paying 1.0%. During the course of Drake's deception, the Clients paid approximately $1.5 million in management fees – over $1.2 million more than Drake represented to the Clients that they were paying – and Drake received approximately $900,000 of those fees as incentive-based compensation.

Taxes

- Deducted excess taxes from client income but paid a lesser amount or none to the government (IRS) and kept the difference;

- Failed to file income tax returns;

Cover-Up

- Advisors repeatedly told clients that their finances were in good shape;

- Advisor didn't provide accurate or useful financial reports that helped clients to understand where their money was going; i.e. personal spending, money that supports an entourage, or who money was paid to. If you aren't receiving reporting that you can easily understand and provides details of how your money was used, the advisor is either incompetent, afraid to deliver bad news or doesn't want you to know what's really going on;

- Bank and/or investment account statements were mailed to the advisor rather than to the client; and clients did not have access to review account activity online;

- Advisors falsified documents such as bank statements, investment statements and contracts, etc. provided to the client. With technology, it is very easy to create almost any type of fake documents.

- Advisors forged signatures of clients on bank and other important documents.

Not all of the above points were associated with exposure to a sudden significant loss. Some were smaller losses or misuse of client money. However, an agent or advisor who is willing to put his interests ahead of yours, or to steal small amounts from you (or from others), or to pay his own expenses with your money, is still dishonest and poses an unacceptable risk to you. Remember this: low $ frauds and thefts just haven't had time to grow into large frauds and thefts, but they will if allowed to continue.

If your agent/advisor is doing anything inappropriate or in any way dishonest with your money, you should make immediate arrangements to cut off their access to your funds and find a new advisor.

Summary

Investing (over longer time horizons) is the only real hope most people have of preserving the wealth you will need to ensure your financial security after you retire. Studies have shown time and again that trading or betting does not beat a sensible investing strategy.

Even with a commitment to investing, you need to be in the right investments. Many of the high risk investment products are discussed above, but since new high risk investment products are being developed on an on-going basis, any list will be incomplete. You need to evaluate each investment opportunity. When you do, some of the characteristics of investments you should avoid include:

- Unregistered or exempt
- No transparency to ensure the money is used as intended
- No prospectus or offering documents
- No liquidity (i.e. your money is locked in for long periods)
- No market for resale so no source to determine real value
- Load fees charged to get into or out of investments
- High fees and operating expenses
- Offshore location

- Complex investment structure
- Private investments in startups, restaurants or similar opportunities
- No independently verified track record
- Classified as High Yield
- Sold as guaranteed or low risk
- No independent custodian involved
- Value is based on tax incentives
- Proprietary products
- Investment is not audited

Conclusion

Preserving your wealth is anything but easy. Ask Sergei Fedorov who lost upwards of $40 million to his (former) friend and advisor; or Antoine Walker who made $110 million but was bankrupt shortly after retiring; or Tim Duncan who recently sued Charles banks, his advisor for close to 15 years, for $20 million; or any of the 30 professional athletes who relied on their advisor Jeff Rubin and lost tens of millions. As illustrated by countless cases, many permanent losses are caused by embezzlement, investment fraud or incompetence.

Key Take Aways

You can't rely on trust to protect you from losses. You must take steps to verify a potential agent, business manager or advisor's character, competence, business practices and controls in place to safeguard your money and investments.

Unfortunately even the money you receive from a big contract doesn't go as far as you may think. Make sure you know how much you will actually receive after paying taxes, agent's commissions, advisor's fees, etc. and what living expenses must be paid. You may still receive a lot but probably not as much as you expected.

Many of the losses discussed above were caused by embezzlement or theft of funds under the advisor's control. If you are allowing one agent or business manager or firm to make investment decisions, manage your finances and do the accounting for your wealth, you are giving them total control and almost unlimited opportunity to take your wealth and hide the losses. Use a team of advisors rather than one firm to do everything. Especially, don't allow a firm with access to your money or investments to do your accounting.

The investment losses suffered by athletes and celebrities were largely caused by investing in private, exempt or unregistered investments offering high returns. If you simply must invest in these types of opportunities, limit your investment to a small percent of your total investments.

No matter the source of any investment opportunity, always ensure thorough due diligence is performed. With technology today, anything can be made to look good on the surface.

To paraphrase Antoine Walker, if you aren't there to watch your money, bad things are going to happen. You and/or your independent representative must monitor what is happening with your money and investments. Are you receiving all of your income? Do you know who and what your money is paying for? What is your money being invested in? Is your financial situation improving or are you growing poorer?

Your advisors may say they monitor your money and investments so you don't need to. But this means they are monitoring their own decisions and actions. Keep in mind that monitoring isn't only watching out for embezzlement or fraud but also for mistakes or mismanagement that your advisors either may not recognize or want to report to you. You're in a business arrangement with your advisors and you have to take the steps necessary to ensure you don't lose what you have. Monitoring of your affairs, whether by you or your representative, is a necessity regardless of your relationship with your advisor and how they feel about it.

References

(1) Getlin, Rand. "Cash-strapped NFL players seeking high-risk "Lockout Loans" ThePostGame.com

http://www.thepostgame.com/features/201104/tpg-exclusive-cash-strapped-nfl-players-seeking-high-risk-lockout-loans

(2) Suttles, Aaron. *"Antoine Walker educates Alabama football team on financial pitfall."* Tuscaloosanews.com

http://www.tuscaloosanews.com/article/DA/20140811/Sports/605152962/TL/

(3) Ibid

(4) Solinsky, Kolby. "At First Take Antoine Walker Tells The Boys How He "Lost" $110 Million" whitecovermag.com

http://www.whitecovermag.com/at-first-take-antoine-walker-tells-boys/

(5) Schoeff, Jr., Mark. "Brokers Warned to Boost Training on Complex Products". InvestmentNews.com

http://www.investmentnews.com/article/20141030/FREE/141039990/brokers-warned-to-beef-up-training-on-complex-products

(6) Pound, Edward T. and Pasternak, Douglas. "How some of the NFL's biggest stars got taken for millions." forums.leagueunlimited.com

http://forums.leagueunlimited.com/threads/show-me-the-money.340390/

(7) Anglen, Robert. "Phoenix financier pleads for leniency in fraud case." azcentral.com

http://www.azcentral.com/story/money/business/2014/07/25/phoenix-financier-pleads-leniency-fraud-case/13189769/

(8) Ain, Howard. "Investment fraud seemed legit." comotvideo.com

http://comotvideo.com/download/QdjjDAS7gOQ/howard-ain-troubleshooter-investment-fraud-seemed-legit/

(9) Browning, Dan. "Money manager faces mom at trial." StarTribune.com

http://www.startribune.com/money-manager-faces-mom-at-trial/150877705/

(10) Cruise, David and Griffiths, Alison. *Net Worth: Exploding the Myths of Pro Hockey*, Toronto, Viking, 1991.

(11) *Stafford, Katrease.* "Sergei Fedorov's ex-manager convicted of fraud" freep.com

http://www.freep.com/story/news/local/michigan/wayne/2015/09/03/sergei-fedorovs-ex-manager-convicted-fraud-joseph-zada/71651184/

(12) Mullen, Liz. "Sleaze factor off the charts, agents allege." sportsbusinessdaily.com

http://www.sportsbusinessdaily.com/Journal/Issues/2002/06/20020624/Special-Report/Sleaze-Factor-Off-The-Charts-Agents-Allege

(13) Isaacson, Melissa. "New Villain: Financial Adviser." articles.chicagotribune.com

articles.chicagotribune.com/2000-03-05/sports/0003050077_1_financial-planners-college-sports-agent

(14) Soshnick, Scott. "Losing $25 Million Won't Decide Whether Spurs' Duncan Returns." Bloomberg.com

http://www.bloomberg.com/news/articles/2015-06-17/losing-25-million-won-t-decide-whether-spurs-duncan-returns?cmpid=yhoo

(15) Carney, John. "Hedge Fund Boss Preying on African-Americans Arrested." CNBC.com

http://www.cnbc.com/id/100792619

(17) Scwed, Fred. *Where are the Customers' Yachts: or a Good Hard Look at Wall Street. New York: Simon & Schuster, 1940*

(18) Mahany, Brian. *UBS Financial Services Accused of Trust Fraud,* The National Law Review, January 28, 2015

(19) Sullivan, T.J. "The Man Behind the Money Pit", VCStar.com

www.vcstar.com/.../the-man-behind-the-money-pit

(20) Pound, Edward T. and Pasternak, Douglas. "How some of the NFL's biggest stars got taken for millions." forums.leagueunlimited.com

http://forums.leagueunlimited.com/threads/show-me-the-money.340390/

(21) Fazzi, Raymond. "Former NAPFA Chair Spangler Gets 16 Years For 'Complete Betrayal." Fa.mag.com

http://www.fa-mag.com/news/former-napfa-chair-spangler-gets-16-years-for--complete-betrayal-17272.html

(22) Pfau, Wade. "Dave Ramsey's 8% Withdrawal Rate." wpfau.blogspot.com

http://wpfau.blogspot.com/2013/06/dave-ramseys-8-withdrawal-rate.html

(23) Cole, Jason and Getlin, Rand. *"Raucous lifestyle leads to fall of Jeff Rubin, former financial advisor to NFL players."* yahoo.com

https://www.yahoo.com/news/nfl--raucous-lifestyle-leads-to-fall-of-jeff-rubin--former-financial-adviser-to-nfl-players-.html

(24) Sommer, Jeff. "A Path to Retirement, for Those Far From It." NYTimes.com

http://www.nytimes.com/2014/05/04/your-money/a-path-to-retirement-for-those-far-from-it.html?_r=0

(25) Valencia, Milton J. "Author Patricia Cornwell awarded $50.9m in suit." Bostonglobe.com

https://www.bostonglobe.com/metro/2013/02/19/mystery-writer-patricia-cornwell-wins-boston-lawsuit/srxHZZC5A9j3MsIBVscsON/story.html

(26) Smith, Steven A. Interview with Antoine Walker, *First Take - Antoine Walker - From $110m To Broke,* ESPN, October 2, 2012.

(27) Mullin, Liz. "Auditor watches Martina's money managers." sportsbusinessdaily.com

http://www.sportsbusinessdaily.com/Journal/Issues/2002/06/20020603/Special-Report.aspx

(28) Glenn, Everett L. "Unsportsmanlike Conduct: The Exploitation of Black Athletes – Part II." atlantadailyworld.com

http://atlantadailyworld.com/2013/12/02/unsportsmanlike-conduct-the-exploitation-of-black-athletes-part-ii/

(29) Schoeff, Mark Jr. "SEC warns investors that advisors could be mishandling assets." Investmentnews.com

http://www.investmentnews.com/article/20130304/FREE/130309972/sec-warns-investors-that-advisers-could-be-mishandling-assets

(30) Evans, David. "How investors lose 89% of gains from futures funds." bloomberg.com

http://www.bloomberg.com/news/articles/2013-10-07/how-investors-lose-89-percent-of-gains-from-futures-funds

(31) Jessop, Alicia. "not-broke-how-nfl-players-stayfinancially-stable-after-the-game-ends." Forbes.com

http://www.forbes.com/sites/aliciajessop/2012/10/31/not-broke-how-nfl-players-stay-financially-stable-after-the-game-ends/

(32) Abshure, Heath. "Congress ignores ticking time bomb of investment fraud." Thehill.com

http://thehill.com/blogs/congress-blog/economy-a-budget/315967-congress-ignores-ticking-time-bomb-of-investment-fraud

(33) Gardner, Eriq. "Hollywood's Business Managers." hollywoodreporter.com

http://www.hollywoodreporter.com/lists/hollywoods-business-managers-187592

(35) Evans, David. "Forex Investors May Face $1 Billion Loss as Trade Site Vanishes." Bloomberg.com

http://www.bloomberg.com/news/articles/2014-11-13/forex-investors-may-face-1-billion-loss-as-trade-site-vanishes

About the Author

Mike Mumford is a CPA, CFF (Certified in Financial Forensics), CFE (Certified Fraud Examiner), and Chartered Professional Accountant - Canada (formerly known as Chartered Account or CA); and has practiced exclusively in the area of forensic accounting, financial investigations and personal financial risk consulting for 30 years.

Mike began his financial career in Canada as an external auditor. After qualifying for his Chartered Accountant designation he took a public accounting position in Bermuda, where the majority of his time was spent performing audits of financial services companies.

Upon returning to Canada, Mike joined the Lindquist Holmes forensic accounting practice in Toronto. This was a unique practice that, at the time, was the sole provider of forensic accounting services to the Royal Canadian Mounted Police and other law enforcement agencies on complex white-collar crime investigations. It was through these criminal investigations that Mike learned what was needed to meet the standard of proof for criminal fraud, how to conduct effective interviews of witnesses and subjects, and how to report and testify on complex fraud, transactions and financial concepts. Mike's experience working with law enforcement on criminal cases included financial institution frauds, Ponzi and other investment schemes, embezzlement, money laundering and proceeds of crime asset tracing. Mike also was frequently retained by financial regulators to perform fraud and conflict of interest investigations at financial institutions and insurance companies.

In 1994 Mike joined Arthur Andersen and became Partner-in-Charge of the Business Fraud Risk Services practice for Canada. In 1997 he moved to the U.S. to start and lead Deloitte's Minneapolis Forensic and Investigative Services practice. In 2002 Mike started his current company, Luminescent Inc., which now does business as FirstRule Financial Inc.

FirstRule Financial provides investigative and forensic accounting services, and also proactively consults with successful individuals, families, family businesses and other related entities to help protect their wealth and financial security. These proactive services include identifying risky financial practices that could cause significant losses, due diligence on advisors and investments, financial education and independent financial monitoring.

Mike can be contacted at Mike.Mumford@FirstRuleFinancial.com.

Appendix 1 – Basic Concepts

This section provides additional detail and explanation of certain terms and concepts, some of which were touched upon earlier.

Longer Life Expectancy

One of the benefits of being alive today is that we all have a longer life expectancy. In 1800 the average life expectancy was around 40 years. In 1900 it was approximately 45. People didn't live long enough to retire so they didn't have to save for after they stopped working.   Today average life expectancy is close to 80. And there's a good chance you'll live to 100 or more. This means that your retirement could be 40 or 50 or more years. How great is that!

Well, it's fantastic unless you run out of money and since you don't know how long you'll live you can't know with any certainty how much you'll need to have saved when you do retire.   Your financial planner should be able to help you figure out a range of what you might need but it won't ever be exact. You can be sure however, that it's a much bigger amount than you would have needed years ago. So you need to be saving now, avoid losing what you save, and investing wisely.

Risk and Return

There are no high returns with low risk. We'd all love to find such an investment. But they don't exist. If someone offers you an opportunity to invest in a "sure thing" with "no risk" or "minimal risk", that's going to earn a high return, you are being scammed or your advisor isn't competent. No doubt, you will be approached by people recommending that you put your money into opportunities with high potential returns, but these will be either highly speculative or fraudulent.

The risk involved investing in something with potential high returns is substantial. Consider the following:

If the opportunity is fraudulent and you invest, your money is gone never to return.

Even if it's a legitimate opportunity with a chance to earn a high return, its high risk means that chances are good that you will lose your entire investment, not just some portion of it.

Risk and return really boils down to this: if a high return investment opportunity is not fraudulent then it's highly speculative; meaning it's not an investment, it's gambling. And if you want to have future financial security, you don't gamble on speculative opportunities.

Inflation

Simply put, money loses its purchasing power over time because of inflation. Inflation means the prices of your purchases increase; so a dollar buys less next year and less again the year after. You can't do anything to stop the costs going up, but a dollar stays a dollar. So in future years you need more dollars to buy the same things you buy today. In 1930 you could buy a bottle of Coke for a nickel, but today a nickel won't buy you much of anything.

While you are still earning income, you can negotiate for a higher salary each year, or if you get paid by the hour you can work more hours to earn more dollars. But the dollars you have already earned and the ones you are saving now will lose purchasing power over the years. This means that you need more dollars this year to buy the same things you bought last year. Since a dollar is still a dollar, in order for your savings keep up with the increasing costs, you need to invest what you have saved to earn more dollars.

The minimum goal of investing while you are still earning income is to earn more from your investments than inflation costs you. This allows you to accumulate more dollars, and maintain your purchasing power, for you when you are no longer earning an income and are living off your retirement savings.

The Power of Compound Interest

Compound interest is the interest you earn on the interest you previously earned but left in the investment.

Compounding interest produces remarkable growth over time. The magic is, the earlier you start investing; the greater the compounding effect will be, so you need to start investing now if you haven't already. By adding to your investments each year, the impact of compounding will create remarkable results.

The following example shows the impact of investing $10,000 each year for 30 years and earning interest at 5% per year, which is left in the account so the interest compounds. The blue shows the growth of $10,000 added each year for a total of $300,000 at the end of 30 years. The red shows the growth of the compound interest earned. By the end of 30 years, the interest you have earned is $397,000 and the money you put in each year (called the "principal") is $300,000, for a total of $697,000.

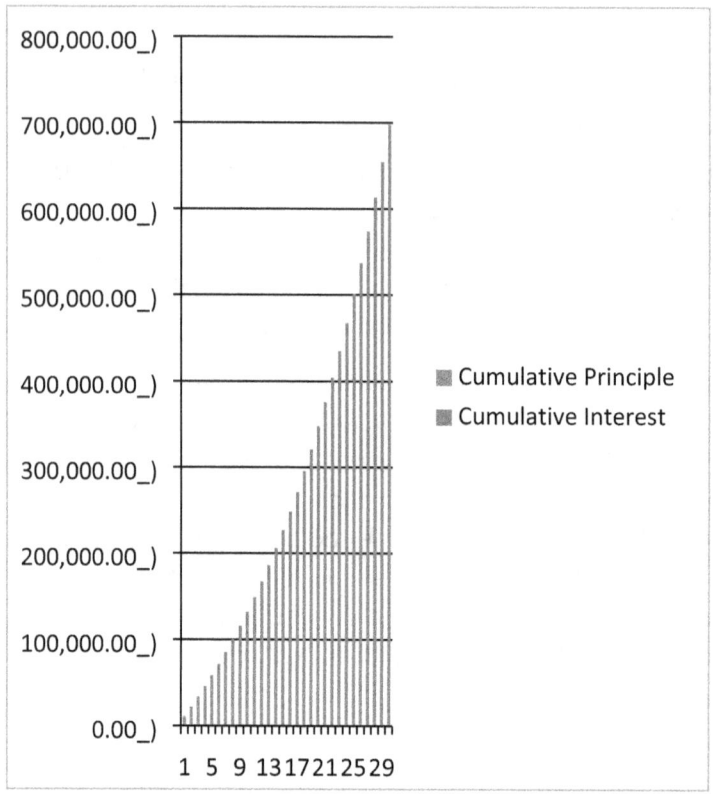

Your contributions at $10,000/year for 30 years $300,000

Compound interest at 5% per year for 30 years $397,607

Total at the end of 25 years $697,607

       This example ignores taxes which you would pay on interest earned unless the investment was held in a non-taxable account.

Dividend Reinvestment

       Shares of some companies pay dividends, which are payments to the owner of the shares. Those dividends can be taken and spent, or they can be reinvested in the same shares. The impact of dividend reinvesting is very much like compounding interest; as shown in the above graph. As you reinvest dividends to acquire more shares, you get more dividends which in turn are reinvested in more shares to get you even more dividends. Over time, the reinvestment of dividends will have a huge positive impact on the growth of your investments.

Income Tax Efficiency

You can own your investments in tax deferred accounts (qualified Individual Retirement Accounts "IRA's") and/or in taxable accounts. Tax deferred accounts allow you to take an income tax deduction in the year you put money into the account, and the money earned in those accounts is not taxed until you take the money out of the account. But when you do take the money out of tax deferred accounts you will be taxed on all of it. Unfortunately, you can only put a limited amount into tax deferred accounts each year. The example of compound interest shown in the chart above assumes you are investing in a tax deferred account.

In contrast, interest or dividends earned on investments owned outside your tax deferred accounts are taxable. You buy the investments with money that you already paid taxes on and then you pay taxes on any interest or dividends that are paid to you on the investments each year. But when you sell these investments, any amount that you have already paid taxes on is yours; you will not pay taxes on the amount you originally invested or on the interest or dividends you have already paid taxes on. Of course if you make a profit on the sale, it is taxable.

It is important to consider whether you will hold an investment in a tax deferred account or outside. You shouldn't need to know which investments are better held in what accounts, but you should make sure that your advisor considers this. It will have a large impact on how much of the earnings on your investments you get to keep vs. give to the government. Over the years, this can have a substantial impact on the growth of your investments.

Let's take the same example of compound interest we used above, but assume you pay personal income tax at 40% of your income.

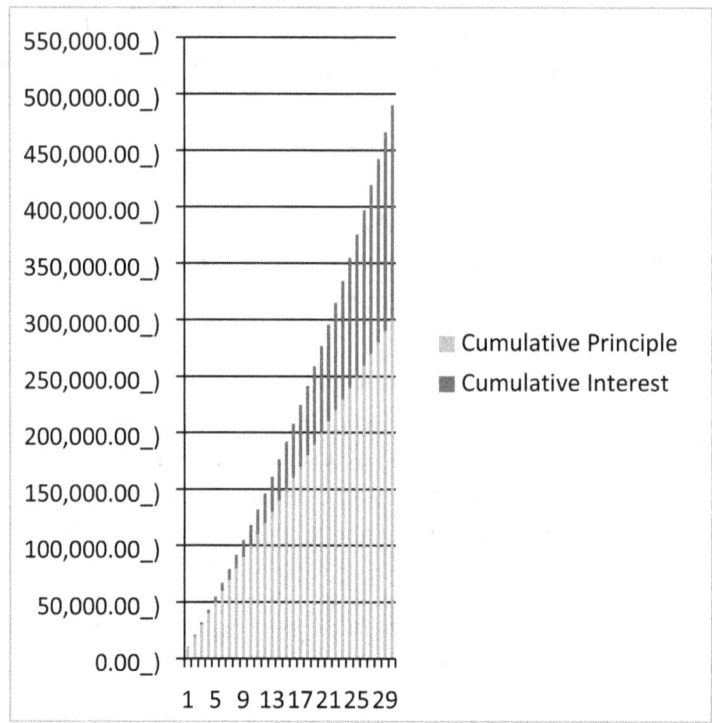

In this case, if the investment income was taxable, the interest grows much more slowly and after 30 years the investment has reached $490,026; compared to $697,607 in a tax deferred account.

Summary

If you don't invest, your savings will definitely lose purchasing power over time. However, all investments are not equal in risk or return. Understanding the basic characteristics of different types of investments is a first step in being able to understand what your advisor is doing or advising you to do. When you tell your advisor you want to be in conservative investments so that you will have money to retire on, you need to know what investments are conservative and which are risky.

Appendix 2 – Who Does What: the Players

There are a few main players, besides your Agent, whose roles you should understand.

- A **Financial Planner** assists you to put together a plan to meet your financial objectives. This may involve some or all of helping to set financial goals, develop income projections and budgets, perform tax, estate and retirement planning, and coordinating with your other advisors. This is a very important role but is not regulated; anyone can call themselves a financial planner or do the work. It is important that the person advising you on your financial plan, whether your agent or another financial advisor, is knowledgeable and competent.

- An **Estate Planner** helps you to set up your financial affairs in a way that minimizes taxes to your estate and beneficiaries when you transfer some of your wealth to others during your lifetime or when you die. Although you might initially think that you wouldn't transfer assets while you are living, this can result in substantial tax advantages to you and your estate while still allowing you to control those assets. This is an area where many wealthy celebrities have dropped the ball, costing them substantially higher taxes over their lifetime and their beneficiaries millions upon their death.

- **Wealth Manager** is a term used by many financial advisors, but has no defined meaning and is not regulated. It doesn't require any specific qualifications and illustrates why you have to dig into a potential advisor's background to know what you are getting when you hire an advisor.

- **Business Manager** or **Financial Manager** are other terms without a defined meaning but is generally someone who manages the financial aspects of actors and other entertainers' lives. A **Personal Manager** manages multiple aspects of an entertainer's personal life which might also include the financial aspects.

- An **Investment Advisor** is anyone who gives you advice on investing your money. But there is an important differentiator that you should pay attention to. Your Investment Advisor should preferably be an **Investment Adviser Representative ("IAR")** who is employed by a **Registered Investment Adviser ("RIA")**. The RIA must be registered either with the Securities & Exchange Commission ("SEC") or a State Securities regulator. An **IAR owes you a fiduciary duty** to put your interests ahead of any others, including their own.

- A **Registered Representative** is employed by a broker-dealer. They may also be known as a broker, stock broker, Account Manager, investment advisor, financial advisor or another term. They also recommend investments but they aren't IAR's and **don't necessarily put your best interests first**. Registered Representatives do not have a fiduciary responsibility to their clients when recommending investments to purchase or sell. In fact, they only have a duty to make *suitable* recommendations to you. **Taking investment advice from someone who does not accept a fiduciary responsibility to put your interests first, before his/her own interests, is a terrible idea.**

- Now, to really confuse things, many Registered Representatives are also registered as IARs. This allows them to help you develop an investment plan as an IAR, but then act as a Registered Representative when recommending investments. Trying to keep track of when the advisor is acting as a Registered Representative without a fiduciary duty to you versus when he is acting as an IAR with a fiduciary duty to you is too confusing to be worth the bother. It also presents a problem if you ever have to try to prove a claim against them for receiving bad advice. In other words, you are well advised not to have a Registered Representative as your investment advisor.

- Do not confuse sales people who come to you promoting a private opportunity to invest in the next big thing, or someone who calls or emails you with opportunities to invest, with investment advisors. These people are generally called either **promoters** or **producers** and are trying to convince you to invest your money, regardless of the merits of the investment; or are con-men. It is very likely that these people aren't registered or regulated and your risk of suffering permanent losses is extremely high if you invest through them or in the products they are selling.

- **Brokerage firms** ("brokers") are the middlemen between the buyer and seller of securities (i.e. stocks, bonds, options). In other words they execute the trades (for a fee) when you buy and sell publicly traded securities.

- **Dealers** are firms whose business is buying and selling securities for their own account (not for others) trying to make a profit by trading securities.

- **Broker-dealers** are firms that are both brokers and dealers. Although you may know, or have been told, the broker-dealer will make a commission on your purchase or sale of investment securities, you may not know that the party you are buying from or selling to may be the same broker-dealer recommending the deal. This presents a conflict of interest if you are being advised by a Registered Representative, not only because of the commission he will earn but also because the stock recommended may be one the broker-dealer wants to dump.

- **Custodians** are firms that hold the investments you purchase, register your ownership, collect interest or dividends earned on your investments and handle the money as directed, and send out account statements to you confirming what is registered in your name. This is an important role; many investment frauds are able to occur because there was no independent custodian holding and reporting the investments.

- **Accountants and/or bookkeepers** maintain your personal financial records that are needed to track financial transactions such as your earnings and deposits, expenses and other payments, purchases and sales you make, and whatever other information is agreed upon. Your accountant should not have access to your money or investments. Some Business Managers are accountants by background but don't let then fill both roles for you.

- **Tax advisors** help to determine how to accomplish certain goals while paying the lowest tax. Tax preparers use information from the accountants and others to prepare your federal and state tax returns, as well as others such as estate and gift returns where appropriate.

- **Insurance brokers and agents** sell insurance. An insurance **broker** is not affiliated with a specific insurance company so will look for the best coverage for you at the best price. An insurance **agent** is employed by or affiliated with a specific insurance company and generally sells only policies from that insurance company.

  Some insurance companies have formed separate broker-dealer companies, resulting in many of their agents becoming Registered Reps as well as Insurance Agents. This allows them to sell securities and annuities in addition to insurance policies; not necessarily a good thing for you.

- **Bill payers** are firms that receive your bills and pay them. To do this, they generally have access to your bank account and can write checks or make electronic payments from your account.

These are the main players you may deal with or hear mentioned in discussions. You will likely run into many others who will want you to buy something or give you advice. As with those mentioned above, never agree to hire or work with them or accept an investment recommendation until you have thoroughly checked them out.

There are numerous references to two main regulators throughout this book. They are

- The **U. S. Securities and Exchange Commission** is often referred to as the **SEC**. The SEC is the federal agency created to protect investors, oversee investment markets and enforce regulations.

- The **Financial Industry Regulatory Agency,** or **FINRA**, is not a government agency but does have authority to write and enforce rules governing broker-dealers and Registered Representatives.

Although there are other regulators, these are the two you are most likely to hear about.

Appendix 3 – Information to Request from Potential Financial Advisors or Managers

Name: _____

Employer(s): _____

Position/Title:_____

Other businesses you are affiliated with and relationship:

_____

Advisor Background

1. Please list all your licenses, with license number, year obtained and regulator.

2. Please list all FINRA exams and year passed.

3. Please list all your degrees, credentials and professional memberships with name of the issuing organization and year obtained.

4. Please list your previous employers or companies you were affiliated with for the past ten years.

5. Have there ever been any complaints filed against you with

   a. Current or past employers?

   b. Regulators?

   c. If so please describe.

6. Have you been sued? If so, please provide details.

7. Have you been recognized as a leader in the industry? If so, by whom and describe what it recognizes?

8. How many clients do you have now and at the year end of the prior four years?

9. How much are your Assets Under Management ("AUM") now and at the year end of the past four years?

10. What is the makeup of your clientele? Describe how it has changed over the last five years.

11. Do you have a specialty that you are known for?

12. Will you provide client references, both current and former, if requested?

13. How are you compensated?

    a. Salary?

    b. Commissions?

    c. Bonuses?

    d. Referral fees?

    e. Other? (explain)

14. Are there incentives for you to recommend certain financial products? If so, please describe.

15. If selected to be my advisor, will you sign a release to allow me or a representative to perform a credit check on you?

Fiduciary Duty

1. Do you acknowledge a fiduciary duty to me in all services you will potentially provide? If not, please describe all exceptions.

Service Providers/Outsourced Services, Business Partners

1. What broker dealer(s) would be used to execute purchases or sales of investments for my account?

2. Describe any compensation you, your employer or business receives from each broker-dealer named.

3. Describe your Custody arrangements.

4. Describe any compensation you, your employer or business receives from each custodian.

5. Describe any compensation or benefits you, your employer or business receives from each asset manager who could be managing any of my money.

6. Who provides administrative back office services to you?

7. Do any other related parties provide services? If so, who and what?

8. Have you done due diligence on each of the above service providers for the following:

    a. Any history of complaints?

    b. Any regulatory issues?

    c. Any lawsuits?

    d. Financial viability?

    e. Insurance coverage?

    f. Privacy and Information Security?

Employer/Affiliated Business Information

1. Is your employer/affiliated business an arm's length party or do have an ownership or other interest in it? If not arm's length, what is your interest?

2. Which of the following services do your employer/affiliated businesses offer?

   a. Financial planning

   b. Budgeting

   c. Cash management

      i. Set up bank accounts

      ii. Receive deposits

      iii. Arrange loans

      iv. Transfer funds

      v. Withdraw cash

   d. Bill paying

   e. Arranging major purchases

   f. Arranging travel

   g. Other concierge services (describe)

   h. Tax planning

   i. Player contract negotiation

   j. Endorsement negotiation

   k. Contract monitoring

   l. Investment selection

m. Investment due diligence

n. Investment purchases and sales

o. Margin loans

p. Other loans

q. Estate planning

r. Philanthropy guidance

s. Charitable administration

t. Family governance

u. Real estate transactions

v. Real estate management

w. Private business management

x. Insurance consulting

y. Insurance products

    i. life,

    ii. disability,

    iii. long-term care,

    iv. health and

    v. property/casualty

    vi. other - describe

z. Education funding

aa. Retirement planning

bb. Accounting

cc. Tax preparation

dd. Other - specify

3. Describe the reporting you provide to clients. Please provide an example.

4. Do you offer assistance with financial plan implementation?

5. Do you take custody of, or have access to my assets? If yes, please describe.

6. Who regulates your employer and/or affiliated business and what are the registration numbers with each regulator?

7. Unless you are employed by a publicly traded company, please describe the corporate structure of your employer including parent, subsidiaries and sister companies.

8. Provide names of the firm's principals and top management and their experience.

9. Who is the Chief Compliance officer?

10. How many employees does your employer/affiliated business have?

11. How long has your employer/affiliated business been operating?

12. Who are your employer/affiliated business' attorneys?

13. Who are your bankers?

14. Is your employer/affiliated business audited and if so by what entity?

a. When was the last audit completed?

15. How much capital does your employer/affiliated business have?

16. Please provide a copy of your employer/affiliated business financial statements.

17. When was the last regulatory examination performed and by whom?

18. What issues, if any, were identified by the examination?

19. Are client accounts insured by SIPC?

20. Do you have error-and-omissions insurance?

    a. Who is your insurer?

    b. How much coverage do you have?

21. Do you have crime insurance to cover embezzlement or employee dishonesty?

    a. Who is your insurer?

    b. How much coverage do you have?

22. Have you had a risk assessment or internal control review by an external party? If so, provide company and date.

23. Have you implemented internal controls and procedures to protect client assets? If so, please provide a copy of the applicable policies and procedures.

24. Do you have an employee hotline or other mechanism that allows anonymous reporting of issues?

25. Have you had any insurance claims against you or your employer/affiliated business or have you notified your insurer of any potential claims? If any, please describe.

26. Who would be involved in managing my account?

27. Do you require "discretionary" trading authority over my investment accounts?

28. Do you request a Power of Attorney? If so, for what purposes?

29. Is there an online account management system that clients can access to see the investments and transactions in their accounts? If so, what is the system?

30. Are there any restrictions on what products you can recommend?

31. Approximately what percentage of your Assets Under Management are in each of the following?

    a. _____% Insurance products

    b. _____% Annuities

    c. _____% Stocks

    d. _____% Bonds

    e. _____% Mutual funds and ETF's

    f. _____% Limited Partnerships

    g. _____% Commodities

    h. _____% Options

    i. _____% Real Estate

    j. _____% Alternative Investments

    k. _____% Coins, tangibles, collectibles

    l. _____% Private placements

    m. _____% Foreign exchange products

n. _____% Other:

_____

o. _____% Other:

_____

32. Do you have online brokerage?

33. Do you provide clients with written information such as a prospectus or offering memorandum for all recommended investments?

34. Do you have third-party endorsements, such as media coverage on the company, the clients and services? Please describe.

35. Do you provide ongoing education to your staff? Please describe.

36. Do you provide education for your clients? Please describe.

37. Do you have a business continuity plan?

38. Would we enter into a written contract? If so, please provide a copy of your standard client contract.

39. Would you allow client accounts and transactions to be independently monitored by my appointed representative?

Conflict of Interest

1. Describe all actual and potential conflicts of interest that could arise if we work together.

2. Do you offer proprietary products?

3. If so, what % of your total AUM is in proprietary products?

4. Does any member of your firm act as a general partner, participate in, or receive compensation from investments you might recommend to me? If so, please provide names and role.

5. What other business interests do you personally have, whether directly or indirectly?

6. Could you receive any other compensation of any sort or anything else of value in connection with the investments, advice or other services you provide to me?

7. If you or your employer/affiliated business receive commissions from products purchased by or for me, are those commissions offset against fees you charge?

8. Please provide a copy of your Conflict of Interest Policy.

Fees

1. Describe all the fees and other expenses I will be paying, if I work with you, and how they will be calculated.

2. Are fees negotiable?

3. Do you or your employer/affiliated business receive referral fees from attorneys, accountants, insurance professionals, mortgage brokers or others? If so, please describe the arrangements.

Soft Dollars and Other Income

1. Does your employer/affiliated business receive soft dollars?

2. From whom, how much and what requirements must be met to receive these?

3. What is your policy regarding soft dollars?

Privacy and Information Security

1. Do you have Privacy and Information Security policies?

2. Who provides your information security?

3. Do you have a data breach response policy?

4. Does that policy require immediate notification to clients?

5. Have you ever had a breach of security? Or a data loss? If so, please provide details.

6. Do you have insurance coverage for breaches of data security? What does it cover and how much coverage do you carry?

Appendix 4 – Researching a Financial Advisor

The following is a high level generic example of the type of research and evaluation that should be performed on a prospective financial or investment advisor or business manager. It is impossible to ensure this covers all potential sources of research since all situations are different. Also, the evaluation results will depend upon the skills and experience of the individual performing that evaluation. For instance, it is often what is missing from the information obtained that identifies important issues.

1. Send the Potential Advisor Information Request (Appendix 3) and evaluate all the responses. It is particularly important that the prospective advisor

   a. Acknowledges a fiduciary duty to you, and

   b. Has no conflicts of interest.

2. Research the **advisors and advisory firms** being considered and compare the information you find to what was provided on the Advisor Information Request. Start with Brokercheck http://brokercheck.finra.org/ which contains information on registered brokers and broker-dealers and registered representatives. If the person or firm you are searching is an investment advisory firm or investment adviser representative, you will be taken to the Investment Adviser Public Disclosure ("IAPD") site.

3. Confirm the advisor

   a. Is licensed

   b. Has had no complaints filed against him

   c. Hasn't changed firms regularly

   d. Hasn't stayed more than a few months at a firm that has a history of complaints

4. The Investment Adviser Public Disclosure ("IAPD") site at http://www.adviserinfo.sec.gov/IAPD/default.aspx

    a. The IAPD provides information on Registered Investment Advisers including

        i. Current employers

        ii. Qualifications

        iii. Registration history

        iv. Disclosure information (complaints, charges, disciplinary actions, lawsuits, etc.)

        v. Registrations

        vi. Industry exams passed

        vii. Professional designations

        viii. Previous registrations

        ix. Employment history

        x. Other business activities

    b. For firms, perform background research on owners, principals and senior management as well as the firm itself.

        i. For firms, the IAPD provides information on

            1. Registration Status

            2. Registrations with states

            3. Whether they are exempt from registration

            4. Information on business operations, size, owners

5. Disclosure information on criminal and regulatory actions. Item 11 of the firm's Form ADV will tell you whether the firm or their employees or related persons have criminal or regulatory records. This is of particular importance to assessing your risk.

  ii. At the same site, find the advisory firm's Part 2 brochure

    1. This includes information about the firm's fees, policies, strategies and relationships.

    2. The Part 2 brochure should be read and assessed for problem areas and also for whether it is consistent with what you have found or been told by the advisor or others.

5. Perform a credit check on the advisor being considered (**after obtaining the advisor's written consent**) for signs of financial problems. Financial problems are often a cause of embezzlement or fraud. You want an advisor who

  a. Does not have excessive debt

  b. Pays debts on time

6. Research the advisor's credentials

  a. Research and evaluate the advisor's professional credentials beginning at http://www.finra.org/investors/professional-designations

  b. Visit the website of the organization giving the credential and evaluate the value of that credential.

7. Research the reputation of the advisor, the firm and its owners, principals and senior management.

   a. Google search – websites, blogs, social media, discussion boards

   b. Media search looking for

      i. Lifestyle issues

      ii. Negative issues

      iii. Unsavory associates

   c. Lawsuit search on Pacer.gov

   d. Professional relationships – research reputations of and issues with

      i. Bankers

      ii. Attorneys

      iii. Auditor or accountant

      iv. Business partners

8. Contact references provided by the advisor to discuss satisfaction with the way services were provided.

      i. Services provided

      ii. Satisfaction

      iii. Disputes

      iv. Reason for leaving

9. Attend at the prospective advisor's office to evaluate consistency of information previously obtained including:

   a. Physical security of premises

b. Existence of personnel and professionalism

When assessing the advisor, consider the responses provided and your interactions with him/her as compared to the information in the book.

If you don't feel able to evaluate the advisor for competence or integrity, consider using a consultant to identify two or more advisors with those characteristics. You can then meet with the candidates to judge who you would be more comfortable working with.

Appendix 5 – Asset Classes

The following points describe the asset classes. Not all of these asset classes are appropriate for individuals but it is worth understanding what they are. Asset classes include:

- **Publicly Traded Stocks** - Within the asset class Publicly Traded Stocks, there are further sub-divisions or sectors. These include:
  - Large Cap, Mid Cap and Small Cap – Essentially the "Cap" refers to the "capitalization" of a company, which is the total value of all its shares. Companies classified as Large Cap are generally worth more than $10 billion each, Mid Cap companies are worth around $2 - $10 billion each, and Small Cap are worth around $300 million to $2 billion each. However, these categories aren't fixed and the values of companies do go up and down.
  - Global, U.S., International – Global companies operate around the world; U.S. companies primarily in the U.S. and International operate in some area outside the U.S.
  - Developed and emerging markets – Developed market companies are those based and operating in the U.S., Canada, parts of Europe, Australia and similar countries that have well developed investor protections. Emerging market companies are those in countries with lower or middle income populations and include most countries of the world.
  - Growth stocks are those of companies that are expected to have higher sales or revenue growth than similar companies and therefore are priced higher than those similar companies.
  - Value stocks are those that are considered to be undervalued compared to similar companies and are expected to increase in value to be at least comparable to their peers.

- Sector stocks are basically industry sectors and include healthcare, technology, retail and manufacturing, among others.

The classifications above don't have to be totally separate from each other. For instance, you can choose Large Cap, Large Cap Growth or Large Cap Value stocks; International, International Large Cap, Mid Cap or Small Cap; etc.

- **Preferred Stock** also represents a share of ownership in a company but has different characteristics than common stock. It's not called preferred because it's a better investment; only because in the event the company goes bankrupt, the holders of preferred stock would receive payouts for their shares (if there was any money left which is doubtful) before common shareholders. The other thing about preferred shares is that they pay a dividend at a fixed rate per share, similar to receiving interest.

- **Fixed Income** – This asset class includes investments that pay interest, usually either at scheduled dates or at the end of the investment term, called the maturity date. On the maturity date the principal (the amount invested) is returned to the investor.
    - Bonds are legal agreements setting out the terms of money loaned to the issuer, either governments or corporations. A bond will specify the interest rate, how and when interest will be paid, and any requirements of the issuer. Bonds are given credit ratings which are intended to indicate the relative safety of a bond. The interest rates are based on the credit ratings.

      These fixed income securities are issued by corporations and by municipal, state and federal governments.

    - There are other investments that offer interest but are not bonds. For example, **Promissory Notes** which are basically written promises to pay you back for money you have loaned to a person or company, with interest. These have a **high risk of permanent loss and frequently fraudulent.**

- **Cash and Money Market** – This asset class is made up of investments that are low risk and can be turned into cash on very short notice. These include such things as:
  - Certificates of Deposit- investments purchased directly through a commercial bank or savings and loan institution. They specify the interest rate, interest payment dates and maturity date. Interest rates are quite low as they are issued by regulated financial institutions.
  - Short term government treasury bills- among the safest investments but because of the low risk they also pay a lower interest rate.
- **Annuities** – These are written contracts issued by insurance companies that promise to pay you a series of future payments. These payments are often called guaranteed but the guarantee is only as good as the guarantor's ability to pay. There are many variations of annuities; some promise payments for a specified number of years, others for lifetime; some payments are fixed and others vary based on how the stock market performs; etc. Generally, if you purchase a basic lifetime annuity, when you die there is no payout to your surviving family members, even if you die shortly after purchasing the annuity. There are many options you can purchase for your annuity, such as having benefits paid to your survivors after you die, but you pay substantial additional fees for these options. It is very important to understand the details and costs of any annuity contract and additional options that you purchase.

Annuities that earn variable returns tied to the performance of certain stocks are generally not good investments because of the high purchase costs and annual expenses. On the other hand, a Single Premium Immediate Annuity ("SPIA") can be a reasonable choice for certain people at the right time. These are governed by the annuity contract and you really need to understand what you are paying for and what you are giving up. As an example, many SPIA's offer payments that will continue as long as you live so if you live to 100, it's a great deal. But if you die one month after you purchase it, the money is gone and nothing is paid to your heirs. The terms can be changed to include different payout options but you need to be sure you are clear about what they are.

- Problems with many annuities include high fees and/or restrictive terms. For example, an annuity may have a long lock-in period, where you can't get your money out for an emergency, unless you pay high redemption charges. Annuities are also often pushed by salespeople, especially to elderly people, because of the high commissions earned by the salespeople.
- **Real Estate** – This includes all types of properties including land, commercial offices and warehouses, residential development and rental, and also things such as real estate operating companies, industrial, health-care, and hotels.

    Specific real estate properties can be purchased or you can invest in a Real Estate Investment Trust ("REIT") which pools investors' money to purchase and manage multiple properties within some set of guidelines. REIT's can also be publicly traded or non-traded. The non-traded REIT's aren't usually a good option for individual investors.

- **Alternative investments** – These are investments that are generally not publicly traded and often utilize concentrated investments, are highly leveraged, and/or use confidential (non-transparent) strategies. In the past, most of these have been restricted to investors with a minimum of $1 million to invest, with some requiring much higher amounts. This is changing and there are now liquid, or publicly traded, alternative funds. Because of their strategies, these are generally high risk and if they are in your portfolio at all, it should be money you can afford to lose.

- o Hedge funds have been the most common of the alternative investments in recent years. They have gotten a lot of attention in media because of high returns some of the hedge funds made for pensions and endowments. Be warned, many more hedge funds have suffered crippling losses (and gone bankrupt) than have succeeded in achieving high returns. Note that the fees these hedge funds charge for accepting your money have been very high, and those fees are charged whether they make money for you or not. When hedge funds do make a profit, they will usually charge you additional fees of 20% or more of the profits they made.

- o Another way to invest in hedge funds is through a Fund of Funds. Here you are investing by pooling your money with many others in an investment fund that invests in several Hedge Funds. These are sometimes referred to as Funds of Fee's or Fees on Fees because of the multiple layers of fees that you pay. This makes it much harder for you to make money because the first profits have to cover the annual fees you pay.

- o Private Equity – Private Equity funds will generally pool funds from investors to purchase all or a controlling interest in one or more companies. The Private Equity companies then use their employees and consultants to try to make the company more profitable so they can then sell it at a higher price. This has been done for years by some wealthy individuals and by Private Equity firms that pool money from many investors.

  The profitability of Private Equity is dependent upon the quality of the firm doing the investing and improving the business' profitability. Investing in

Private Equity also has high fees whether profitable or not. You also will have to agree to invest your money for a minimum period of time, usually several years, before you can request it back.

- **Collectibles** – These have become more common as investments in recent years. They include such things as paintings and other art, coins, wine, and anything of value that is in demand. These are very challenging as investments because of counterfeiting, limited resale markets and changes in public taste.
- **Commodities** – These include such goods as precious metals (gold, silver etc.), lumber, oil and natural gas, minerals and farm products. Most investors in commodities do not ever take possession of the physical goods, instead buying and selling contracts for future delivery of those goods (aka futures).

  The commodities market is very high risk for individuals. Many of the companies whose operations create the demand for commodities are very sophisticated and monitor conditions around the world and around the clock to try to anticipate what way prices may go, so being on the other side of trades or contracts with these players is usually going to be very costly. In addition, because of the size of the contracts, you are likely to have to borrow funds to leverage your investment. As said earlier, using leverage can quickly create losses in excess of the funds you had invested.

- **Foreign Exchange (FOREX or FX)** – Because currency of different countries constantly change in value against other countries' currencies, there are opportunities to purchase foreign currency and hold it, hoping it increases in value; or to trade currencies, attempting to make profits on trades.

  Forex trading firms may offer to allow you to invest in this market through them. They claim that since it is a complex area and they are profitable professionals, often with special software tools, they will take your money and trade for you in a managed account. As mentioned earlier, these are often scams.

- **Private Businesses** – There are thousands of private businesses of all sizes that are bought and sold every year and thousands more that are started. It is possible to purchase and run a business or become an investor in one. They may be stand alone or be a franchise. Because the success or failure of these businesses requires a lot of personal time and/or strong management and oversight, they aren't for people who don't have the time or interest to be personally involved.

The following sections discuss some of the frauds and scams that you could be exposed to right now or in the future. These are not types of investments you will be offered. They are descriptions of ways people will try to get you to buy what they are selling.

Appendix 6 – Common Schemes

The following are some of the most common schemes used to separate you from your money:

Affinity fraud – As mentioned earlier, an affinity is a feeling of closeness and trust between people that is often used as an opening to start to build trust with people; with the goal of getting them to pass over money for investments or some other purpose. This has been particularly successful with church congregations but has been used in many other situations such as social clubs, sports organizations, etc.

Ponzi – Lately you can hardly look at the news without reading about a new Ponzi scheme being uncovered. A Ponzi scheme is an investment fraud where investors are promised attractive returns but then their money is not actually invested as they were told. Instead it is used to pay expenses, support a lavish lifestyle and to pay interest to the earlier investors. But then even more new investors have to be found to pay the promised returns to the growing list of old investors. Often, the first investors, upon being paid, start telling others about what a great investment it is. Of course, the scheme falls apart if the fraudsters can't continue to recruit new investors. Some of these Ponzi schemes have gone on for 10 years or more.

Pump and Dump – This scheme involves manipulation of penny (or microcap) stocks to drive up the price (the pump) along with spreading a story about the company's great prospects. When the promoters have created enough buzz to drive up investor demand and the stock gets to a high enough price, the fraudsters sell the shares they had previously bought at a low price (the dump). With the fraudsters bail out, the investors are left with stock that nobody wants. A pump and dump is often carried out by coordinated and well-funded organized crime groups.

Unsolicited Offers – As seen in the movies Boiler Room and American Hustle, **boiler rooms** are literally rooms full of sales people phoning numbers on lists of sales leads, using high pressure sales tactics to sell worthless stocks. These sales people won't give up until you agree to buy or you just hang up.

Going a step further, for any form of **telemarketing**, whether for product or service where you are asked to give any personal information, hang up. Don't buy, don't give credit card or other information, don't confirm personal information. You won't miss out on anything of any value.

Another way criminals will send out unsolicited offers is through **email**. These are more dangerous than telemarketing because simply clicking on a link or downloading an attachment can give the sender access to the information on your computer or the information you type, say when logging on to bank accounts, including your user names and passwords.

Today's Headlines – Without a doubt, when some major economic development is making the headlines, a series of fraud schemes built around that headline will soon follow. For example, when the success of fracking in North Dakota made the news, opportunities to invest in new companies (supposedly) set up to service the wells and the workers were offered everywhere. A similar thing happened with the approval of medical marijuana; new opportunities to invest in grow operations, mostly scams, suddenly "sprang up". Other events over the past few years that spawned their own fraud schemes have included:

- Distressed real estate,
- Hurricanes and other catastrophic weather events, and
- Zika virus cures.

Advance Fee Fraud – These scams generally involve a call or email from someone pretending to be from some business or organization, telling you that they have something of great value for you but that you must first send them a fee so they can release the goods to you. This doesn't have to involve investments but certainly can. As an example, one scam said that the target was entitled to unclaimed war bonds, but they had to send funds up front before the bonds could be sent. Of course, after you send the money, you don't get what you were promised.

Pre-IPO Scams – When companies are going to become publicly traded, they sell shares in what is called an Initial Public Offering or IPO. In the past, there was a trend that when shares were first publicly sold, they quickly went way up in price so there was an opportunity to get rich quick. Scam artists have taken this further by claiming that they could get shares before an IPO occurred. If you bought the shares, you were supposedly in on the ground floor of a stock about to jump in price; pretty much a sure thing. As usual if it sounds too good to be true, it is.

Investment loss recovery scams – There appears to be a market for names of people who have been victims of scams. Once you have been conned in one scheme, it is not unusual to be targeted by other scammers promising they can help you recover your losses. The catch is generally that you have to pay up front for their assistance. All you get in the end is a bigger loss.

Appendix 7 – Questionnaire for Investments Being Considered

Request your advisor to complete the following questionnaire for all new investment recommendations:

- Amount of investment being considered

- Description of investment

- Asset Class

- Is this investment registered, exempt or unregistered?

- If registered, provide details

- If exempt, explain basis of exemption

- If unregistered, explain why it is being considered

- What is the credit agency rating of the investment product or issuing company?

- How does it fit with my investment strategy?

- Reason for its purchase now?

- What is the expected rate of annual return?

    ____% Dividends   ____% Interest   ____% Appreciation

- Will interest or dividends be re-invested?

- What and how much are the fees involved in the purchase?

- What are the annual fees paid to the asset manager or others to maintain the investment?

- What are the restrictions on redemption or resale?

- What other investments did you consider and compare this to?

- Why should I invest in this product over others compared?

- Was due diligence performed? By whom?

- What risks were identified?

- Please provide the due diligence report

- Are there any liquidity restrictions

    o   Restrictions on trading?

    o   Lockup period?

    o   Fees to sell or redeem?

    o   Other restrictions?

- Is the investment subject to capital calls? If so, please explain

- What are the custody arrangements?

- Do you, your firm or the investment issuer or manager have any relationship to the custodian?

- When making this investment, who would my investment funds be paid to?

- Provide details of any regulatory issues the investment, issuer or manager had in the last ten years.

- Provide details of security, if there is any, for the investment.

- Is the investment covered by SIPC?

If the proposed investment is publicly traded please provide the following:

- Securities identifier

- Issuer

- Price range over the past year
- Listing Exchange(s)
- OTC listed?
- Date listed
- What is the investment's maximum drawdown?
- Average daily trading volume

If the investment is not publicly traded please answer or provide the following:

- Description of investment
- Legal entity type of the issuer i.e. Corporation, LLC, LLP, etc.
- Corporate organization structure
- Where is the issuer registered?
- Provide a history of the issuer and the investment
- Provide names of the principals and details of their participation in the investment
- What was the amount and source of the issuer's initial capital?
- What is the issuer's financial position?
- What was the issuer's profitability for last five years?
- Please provide financial statements and projections.
- Is the investment audited? If so by whom?
- How is the investment being marketed?

- Who are the promoters?

- What are the investment risks?

- What is the maximum drawdown?

- Is the investment secured?

- If so, what is the security and is it registered? Obtain details.

- How much could I lose permanently?

- What are the tax implications of the investment?

- How is it valued?

- Who performed the valuation?

- Does it have an investment rating? If so, what is it?

- Who is the Custodian?

- Is the Custodian independent?

- Is the investment held in client name or street name?

- What currency is it in?

- If there is a counter-party, who is it and what due diligence has been performed on it?

- Is the investment insured? If so, by whom?

Additional questions if the investment opportunity is in a private business such as a restaurant, bar, real estate development, etc.

Since a private business often has little history or physical assets, the capability and integrity of the people involved are likely what you are really investing in. These are very risky investments.

- What is the business and its legal structure?

- What is the structure of the investment that is being considered?

    - Is it an investment in shares of the company or is it a loan?

    - If in the shares of the company, what share class and what are the rights and restrictions?

    - If a loan, what are the terms and what is the security?

- What due diligence has been performed on the owners and management?

- What is the source of the startup capital the owners have invested?

- If the owners' contributions were not in cash, what were the contributions and how were they valued?

- What has been done to assess the business's viability? Please provide copies of any studies or other documentation.

- If the business has been operating, what is its record of profitability? Obtain copies of financial statements.

- Does it have a business plan and projections? Are they realistic?

- Besides this investment, how much other money is being raised? Will it be on the same terms?

- Exactly how will the money invested be used?

- Who are the professional advisers; consultants, bankers, accountants, and attorneys?

For All Types of Investments

- How much commission are you paid for selling this product?

- How much commission is your employer paid for selling this product?

- Is any commission or fee of any type paid to a person or entity related to or associated with you or your employer? If so, please provide details including amount and receiving party.

- Are management or other fees paid by the investee to a person or entity related to or associated with you or your employer? If so, please provide details including amount and receiving party.

- Please provide a copy of all offering documents.

Appendix 8 – List of Financial Documents to Retain

The following is a starting list of documents that you should retain (unless they don't apply to you). The list is not necessarily comprehensive of all documents relevant to managing your financial affairs. If you work with a financial advisor, you should request him/her to review and customize it to your particular circumstances. For each document you have, indicate the date the document was created or last updated.

Document

Personal Financial Plan

Budget

Copies of personal financial statements or other reports from your financial advisors

Account account opening documents and most recent statements for all:

- Bank accounts

- Investment accounts

Documentation for all investments whether held in investment accounts or outside, including

- Offering memoranda and similar documents

- Prospectuses

- Trade confirmations

- Proof of Ownership Documents

- Annual Reports, tax returns, and other agreements for private businesses

- Business Operating Agreements

- Annuities prospectuses and contracts

- Inventory of art and ownership documentation

- Inventory of other collectibles and ownership documentation

- Proof of ownership of Intellectual Property

- Deeds and mortgages for all properties owned

- Leases (as lessor or lessee)

- Loan applications and agreements for outstanding loans

- Employment contracts

- Contracts for endorsements and all other sources of earnings

- Retirement Plan Contract(s) and statements

- Contracts with all advisors, business manager, agent, etc.

- Current Will

- Estate plan

- Trust Agreement(s)

- Power(s) of attorney given

- Power(s) of attorney received

- Divorce, separation and nuptial agreements

- Safety Deposit Box Location

- List of contents of Safety Deposit Box

- List of usernames and passwords for online accounts

Insurance applications and policies or declarations pages for

- Life insurance policies

- Disability insurance policies

- Health insurance policies

- Long Term Care policies

- Automobile insurance policies

- Homeowners' insurance policies

- Personal umbrella insurance policies

- Other insurance policies

Income tax returns for at least three years

Estate tax returns

Gift tax returns

www.ingramcontent.com/pod-product-compliance
Lightning Source LLC
Chambersburg PA
CBHW070329220526
45467CB00001B/89